God's Kaleidoscope

Life on the mission field,
in the red light district
and beyond

George Falconer

D0280874

Onwards and Upwards Publishers

Berkeley House,
11 Nightingale Crescent,
Leatherhead,
Surrey,
KT24 6PD,
United Kingdom

www.onwardsandupwards.org

Copyright © George Falconer 2015

The right of George Falconer to be identified as the author of this work has been asserted by the author in accordance with the Copyright, Designs and Patents Act 1988.

All rights reserved.

No part of this publication may be reproduced or transmitted in any form or by any means, electronic or mechanical, including photocopy, recording or any information storage and retrieval system, without permission in writing from the author or publisher.

Printed in the UK by 4edge Limited.

ISBN: 978-1-910197-70-7
Cover design: LM Graphic Design

Scripture quotations are taken from the Holy Bible, NEW INTERNATIONAL VERSION © 1973, 1978, 1984 by International Bible Society. Used by permission. All rights reserved.

Endorsement

As I went through this book I had a great affirmation in my heart. This book is from the Lord. This book is greatly needed. In such an important way it shows how God can use those whom some people call 'just ordinary', when they have a personal relationship with an extraordinary God through His son, the Lord Jesus. Please don't just read it but get copies to pass on to others.

George Verwer
Founder of Operation Mobilisation

Contents

God's Kaleidoscope

Introduction

"Paint me as I am, warts and all."

Oliver Cromwell

"Getting married is the second most important decision you will ever make." So someone said to me. If getting married is only the *second most* important decision, what is the *most* important?

The answer took me from my home town Dunfermline, one of the ancient capitals of Scotland, to the red light district of Amsterdam where I met all kinds of people from all over the world, including a former witch, travellers, prostitutes, and homeless young people. They were all people with a great need. I had the answer to that need for I had had the same need myself.

As a child did you ever look into a kaleidoscope? I did. I loved it. It is like looking into a telescope and seeing only colours. All the colours together make a pattern, and by turning some parts of the cylinder the pattern changes. If one keeps turning it seems that there is no end to the patterns that can be made: some light, some dark, some enchanting and some very surprising. Some seem very soothing and others very stimulating, and the more one looks, the more fascinating it becomes. One never knows what the next pattern will be. Life events are just like the colours, full of surprises. Some are pleasant, some not, some do not seem good at the time but prove to be good in the long run – yet all are unexpected. All of the colours of my life have blended together forming the person I now am.

George Falconer

God's Kaleidoscope

1

Death to Life

I was born two weeks later than expected in the mid-1950s. The maternity staff told my mother that they thought I was dead. To say that to any young woman is something they would surely do hesitantly. I believe, therefore, that they must have been certain that I was indeed dead to say anything at all.

I have often wondered what thoughts went through my mother's mind that day. She would have hoped against hope that they were wrong, but probably thought that with all their experience they would be right. Her older sister had suffered a still birth some years prior, so it is likely that, for a time, my mother may have thought that the same fate had befallen her. In this case the staff were wrong and I came into this world a healthy and very much alive child.

I was the first of two children. I cannot remember our first home, but I know that it was an attic in my grandparents' house. My parents were second cousins. My father came from Rutherglen and my mother was a native of Dunfermline. My father's father had been in the army for twenty-five years, after which he married and had six children, one girl and five boys. Both of my father's parents were dead by the time he was fourteen years old. He went to Dunfermline to work laying pipes and, as he already had relatives there, he stayed with them in the attic; when my parents married, my mother moved into the attic with him. My mother's father was a coal miner at Comrie pit. He was also what was known as a 'knocker upper' which meant that one of his duties was to call at the homes of other miners and knock on the door to make sure that that they were up and ready to go and do their shifts.

The house was not just home to them, it was also a business. It was a boarding house where my grandmother was host to guests who were appearing at the local Opera House. This was a grand-sounding name for a building that was in fact a music hall. Many of the guests who stayed at the house were the dancers, but some of them were top-of-the-bill stars.

My grandparents kept two dogs – spaniels. If any dancer came back with a young man who attempted to get up the stairs to the bedrooms, the dogs stood like guards to prevent this happening. One young man had his trousers torn as he attempted to go up the stairs with a dancer. A dog tried to stop him by biting into his trousers and they ripped. He was so angry!

My grandmother had a rule about the guests who were to be admitted. "First come, first served," she would say. This sometimes led to arguments as those appearing at the opera house would arrive in the town, put their luggage off at the opera house and run to the guest house hoping to get there in time to get a room. Failure to get there quickly enough meant they had to find somewhere else to stay.

There was one exception to the rule. My grandmother would always prepare a room when she knew that Lex McLean was appearing at the Opera House. I can remember seeing him on television when I was a small boy. He was a major comedy star. Winifred Atwell, the pianist, also a major box office star, stayed with them as did the family of Jimmy Logan whom I remember as a comedy actor and leading light in Scottish theatre. I think the guest house was the closest one to the opera house and it was this that led to the competition to stay there.

My father's job came to an end, and to remain in Dunfermline he had to get another, one that he could easily walk to because he did not have a car. Dunfermline was noted for the production of textiles. There were a number of factories in the town that produced these, and he got a job as a despatch foreman at one of them. As I grew up, from time to time he would invite me to come and work with him in the factory. In this way, I got to see what my father actually did for a living. He also had responsibility for the security of the factory, and would go out at night to make sure that it was safely locked up and the alarm set.

We moved out of the attic into a council house. On one side was an old lady and her daughter Doris; we became good friends with the family. On the other side lived a Spanish lady, her Scottish husband and their three daughters. There was a connecting gate between our backyards and they could come through it to play with me and vice versa. There were a couple of steps down from the back doors of the houses. It was across these steps that the girls and I would put two planks of wood. One of the planks was for sitting on and the other we put stones on. We pretended that the stones were sweets and that we were running a shop. I was the shopkeeper and the girls were the customers. I was a happy child.

Like many working class families, the lack of a car meant that we travelled on buses, except for the occasional trip in a taxi when it was necessary such as travelling to the railway station when we were going on holiday. It seemed that every time we required a taxi, we got the same driver.

One taxi ride in particular was significant. On this occasion, I travelled in the taxi with my father to the maternity hospital, knowing that we would return with my mother and the new baby I had been told about. I had threatened my parents by saying that if it was a girl then that was okay, but if it was a boy then I would "put him in the bucket", meaning he would go out with the household rubbish. Upon arrival, my mother came out carrying the baby and got in the front seat of the car. My father said, "Look at the baby, George." I leaned over and saw my brother Jim for the first time lying in our mother's arms fast asleep. I never did put him in the bucket...

One winter we had burst pipes. The entire house was soaked, except for one room: the living room. As it was the only dry room, we had to sleep in it. The couch was a double divan which means that it folded out into a double bed which my parents slept in. I was a small child, so I was able to sleep in my brother's cot, and he slept in his pram. My parents saw to it afterwards that the pipes were lagged so that this never happened again.

When we got our first television set, I spent each afternoon watching The One O'Clock Gang. I loved listening to Dorothy Paul sing on the show and the comedy antics of Larry Marshal and Jimmy Nairn. I also watched Andy Pandy and Bill and Ben the Flower Pot Men.

I adored my Aunt Chrissie. She was a matriarchal figure who loved her family and we loved her in return. When she came to visit, she always bought Smarties for us, chocolate sweets in a tube. Her husband was a driver on the railway which entitled her to reduced cost travel on the trains and this enabled her to visit us as often as she did. She had married at nineteen, just before the Second World War. Her husband Tommy was in the commandoes. He had become a prisoner of war and somehow he had escaped. We all knew in the family that we were not to bring the subject up. It was a difficult time for him and he was badly affected by it. I have always been thankful that all my family survived the war. There were millions who did not.

2

Early Church Experiences

My family went to a congregational church. I thought it old-fashioned, frightening and out-of-date. I did not like being in the sanctuary, which is the main part of the building. My father used to take me into the hall and sit with me until the Sunday school came in. One day he took me into the sanctuary and stood me on a pew. I looked round at all the people and I panicked. I cried as loud as I could. I was terrified.

On another occasion, my brother's christening, my father took me into the sanctuary again and stood me on a pew, as he had previously done, and once more I started to cry. Then I saw my Aunt Chrissie there with her husband and both of their sons. I knew immediately that they had to have made a special trip from their home in Edinburgh. I controlled myself, stopped crying and settled down. From that day on, I was able to go into the sanctuary without bursting into tears.

Like most children, I enjoyed colouring in books at Sunday school, but I never liked the songs. I thought they were old and boring and that was my impression of church. This impression lasted for a long time. The good thing Sunday school did for me was to make me familiar with the stories of the Bible. I found that the man called Jesus was in it, that same person whom my mother told

13

me owned all the birds. I still had no idea who he was, but at Sunday school I found out that he had twelve disciples and he worked miracles.

Sunday school did one thing that I loved. They had an annual concert for the congregation, and the church hall had a platform that was used as a stage. At the time, The Black and White Minstrel Show was very popular on television. We sang songs from it and we had to wear grey shorts, white shirts and black, shoe-lace style bow ties. I loved dressing up and singing. Any excuse to be on stage was a delight to me. On another occasion I devised a puppet show based on the Old Testament story of Isaac and Rebecca, of how they met and married. My interest in doing this was all about the performance. Any story would have done as long as I got to perform. I had a book that I had received from Prize-giving Sunday that taught me how to do some magic tricks. I used this as yet another excuse to do a public performance. The execution of the tricks was somewhat clumsy, but I did not care; I was on the stage and I was performing. As I got older I took performing more seriously. This was to serve me well later in life.

Mr Gahagan, the minister, was a good storyteller. He first told stories to his own children. They would ask him to tell the same tales again and again. In this way he learned to use the same words every time. If he did not, his daughters would stop and correct him. He used the same technique when telling stories publicly. I expect that it is for this reason that two of them stand out in my memory and I have come to appreciate the significance of both.

He told a story about a boy who made a boat. He carved it and lovingly painted it blue and put sails on it. He had spent so much time making it that he loved it and longed for the day when it would be finished and he could sail it. Finally the task was completed and he could do just that. He clutched the boat, ran to a large lake, erected the sails and put it in the water. He watched it sail along the bank as he ran alongside it. However, the wind picked up and the boat sailed out into deep water where he could not reach it, and it sailed out of sight. It was lost. All his hard work and love had been poured into it, and now the boat was gone.

Several weeks passed, until one day the boy was passing by a shop and he saw a boat in the window. As he looked at it, he thought that it looked just like *his* boat. He looked carefully at every detail and shouted, "That is *my* boat!" He ran into the shop and told the shopkeeper. But the shopkeeper said that it was not his. It was for sale and if he wanted it then he had to buy it and only then would it be his.

The boy was disappointed, but he ran home as fast as he could and took out his piggy bank. It was very heavy as he had been saving up coins for a long time. He opened the bank and poured out the coins and counted them. There was just enough to buy the boat. He put the money in a bag, ran back to the shop and paid for it. Then he come out clutching it and excitedly said, "You are mine! You are mine twice over! You are mine because I made you, and now you are mine because I have bought you."

The point of the story is that God has made us, and for those who trust in Jesus he has bought us back again. I did not really understand that at the time, but I do now.

A second story he told concerned the devil and his demons. One day the devil called a meeting of all the demons. He told them that he was fed up with people believing in Jesus. He said that nothing they did could stop some people believing in him.

One demon put his hand up, stood up, and said, "I know what to do. I will go throughout the world starting wars. People will hate and kill one another and then no one will believe in Jesus.

"Sit down," said the devil. "We have tried that before. People still believe in Jesus. We need a new idea. "

Another demon put his hand up, stood up and said, "I know what to do. I will go through all the world and whisper in people's ears, saying that it is not true: 'Jesus did not die for you. He was not real. He has not paid the penalty for sin.' Then no one will believe in Jesus."

"Sit down," said the devil. "We have tried that. It does not work. People still believe in Jesus."

Then the smallest demon stood up and said, "I know what to do. I will go through the world and tell people it *is* true. I will tell them that it *is* true that Jesus is the Son of God, that he was born of the virgin Mary; that he *did* grow up, that he *did* die on the cross for their sins, he *did* rise from the dead and that they can follow him, if they believe in him. Then I will say, 'There is plenty of time.' When they are young, I will say, 'There is plenty of time.' When they grow up, get jobs, marry and have children of their own, I will say, 'There is plenty of time.' They will grow old and I will say, 'There is plenty of time.' Then, when they will reach the end of their lives, it will be too late."

"Then go," said the devil, "and do as you have said."

So all the demons went out telling people there is plenty of time.

I knew that whatever the point of the story was, it meant acting now. I did not do that there and then, but I have come to appreciate the significance of the tale. The Bible says, "...*now* is the ... day of salvation."[1] I was taking a risk!

---

[1] 2 Corinthians 6:2, emphasis added

3

Little School

The day came when I had to start school. If life is a kaleidoscope then the colour of school would be brown. Dark, dreary and unappealing. School was awful. In a short time it seemed that I had a number of different teachers and I found that disturbing. So much so that on one occasion I wet myself in class one day when I was standing in a queue at the teacher's desk to do some reading. It was humiliating. It was a modern school and yet the manner in which lessons were conducted was so Victorian: 'Speak when you are spoken to and know your place' was the order of the day.

The headmistress, however, was a kindly woman. One day when she was taking the class, she told me off for making a mistake in my work. She walked up and down the aisle, came to my desk, looked over my shoulder at my work and then cuffed me over the back of the head. She then walked back to the front of the class. Meanwhile I burst into tears. She paused. I think she was waiting for me to stop crying, but I could not. So after a couple of minutes, she directed her gaze at me, then came up to my desk and comforted me.

Arithmetic was taught by using coloured rods of different lengths as a visual aid. These rods were kept in boxes and handed out to the class. One of the boxes got damaged and when the teacher asked who did it, one boy pointed at me and I was blamed. In fact I knew nothing about how it got damaged. The teacher was very angry. She fixed it with tape and then showed me what she had done to repair it, reinforcing the blame on me. I felt awful being blamed for something that I had not done. It was my first experience of false accusations.

The school had a gym, and I found that I was not good at sport. We were required to climb up ropes. I started to climb and got halfway up but found the stress of trapping the rope between my feet too much for my muscles. The teacher took hold of the rope and swung me back and forth very gently. "Someone wants to go for a swing," she said. Somehow I knew that I was not going to get to the top and no matter how hard I tried, I never did.

I did not make friends at that school. I was alone. But I had not had difficulty making friends before I started school. Perhaps it was the atmosphere there, plus that fact that I was only five years old and had so many teachers in six months, that made me feel that I could not settle down.

I was not aware that school did not have to be as miserable as it was, for I knew no other school. It was like being in a wilderness, a barren, inhospitable place, of which there seemed no end. One can either refresh a wilderness by irrigating it with water, or by leaving for it for fresh pastures. Luckily my family took me to fresh pastures.

My parents decided to move house, and I would have to change schools. The new house was at the opposite end of the town not far from where my grandfather and aunt lived. It was decided that they would live with us. The new house was much larger, and on the other side of the road was a general merchant, a butcher and a small park where children could play.

The new school was so refreshing for me, although things did not go well at first. Changing schools at such a young age was traumatic. At the new school they had also learned arithmetic by using the coloured rods, but the class I was in had made more progress in learning and had stopped using them; they were now doing mental arithmetic. I found it impossible to catch up. This must have been communicated to my parents and, in consultation with the headmistress, it was decided that I would change classes and be moved back six months. This was both a blessing and a curse. It meant starting school all over again. It was a blessing because I could use the rods again, but it was a curse because I remained six months behind for all the years I was there. My new teacher was Mrs Hunter, a stout older lady who clearly had vast experience of teaching. I could not say that I warmed to her but at least she was there every day. She taught the class very well indeed.

From time to time, we would be called into the headmistress's office and told to take our reading books with us. We would form a queue and one by one she made us read passages from our books. As a child I did this because I was told to. I now realise that it was a way of checking our reading skills to find out if remedial work was needed.

For assembly the headmistress would play the piano as we sang hymns. We seemed to sing, "All things bright and beautiful, all creatures great and small. All things wise and wonderful, the Lord God made them all," over and over again. I still did not know who God was but according to that hymn, whoever he was, he made everything. My new school was older than the one I had left. The buildings were Victorian but I felt more settled in it. I made friends. Not many, but I did make a close friend and some others. I would no longer stand alone in the playground as I had at my previous school.

I began being interested in singing and drama at school. In the corner of every room was a box with a speaker in the middle of it. On a fixed day and time the teacher would turn the knob to switch it on and we would hear our music programme. Each term we had music books to follow the lessons. We would sing out loud when told to by the presenter. This was the main way we learned the tunes, but there were other points in the week when teachers would lead the class using the same book while she accompanied us on the piano. Sometimes she would play, "All things bright and beautiful," again. When I sang that hymn, the sun seemed to shine in my heart, even if it was raining outside.

We also had religious education on the radio. Each Thursday morning the teacher would turn the radio on and we would hear the lesson for the day. It was always a Christian theme. Two things stood out to me. There was a series of plays about an alien from outer space called Zed. He would observe humanity and ask questions such as, "Why do people clasp their hands and close their eyes in church?" It was explained that people do this when they are talking to God. Sometimes his observations were amusing. It was to make us think and ask questions. The second thing that stands out was a play based on an imaginary conversation between Reuben and Joseph. In the Old Testament, Reuben was the oldest of the twelve sons of Jacob, and Joseph was the eleventh. They were looking back over the years – how the brothers had sold Joseph into slavery and yet how this had been God's will, because in doing so, they had sent Joseph ahead where, unbeknown to them, he was to become the Prime Minister of Egypt and deliver them in terrible times of famine. I was already familiar with this story from Sunday school but for many other children who did not go to church this would have been very new. Thus it was that I became familiar with Bible stories both at school and Sunday school.

The classrooms had numbers on the doors, one to five. We knew we were moving up the school as we changed classrooms, but Mrs Hunter remained my teacher until the time came to move to the 'big school'.

4

Big School

My first teacher in the 'big school' was Mrs Wilson. Like Mrs Hunter, she was an older lady with a lot of teaching experience behind her. She was a kindly woman with a lovely smile. I enjoyed talking to her. She encouraged us to use our imaginations and write plays. She also expected us to keep diaries. I was so glad to have Mrs Wilson as my teacher, because the class I would have been in was next door and every day we heard their teacher shouting. Mrs Wilson ignored this and I was glad that the shouting teacher was not my teacher as I would have found that frightening. Looking back, I now believe that that teacher was having a nervous breakdown. What I do know is that she left the school and never returned.

There was a room in the 'big school' that was used as an assembly hall, dining room and gym. So much of my life was spent in that room. The plays we wrote were performed in it for the whole school to see. I loved performing. We also went to the same room to watch schools' television programmes.

At playtime my friends and I would play Japs and Commandos or Cops and Robbers such as we saw in Hollywood films. The outside steps to the cellar would become a trench, or walls of the outside toilet would become a defence against attack; there seemed no limit to our imaginations.

There was one boy in my class called David. His family lived in a house by the junction opposite our house. Sometimes I would go and play with him in his family's back garden. David was a very creative boy. As a hobby he wrote sketches which he performed at school. These tended to be one-man sketches based on a pet shop and he performed the part of the shopkeeper interacting with the animals that existed only in his imagination. I loved watching him do this. His scripts were always funny and the whole class enjoyed it. I envied him as I would love to have written and performed sketches like that. It became an occasional and regular fixture that he would be asked to perform these in the class. As he lived across the road from us, I got to know him outside of school and we would play at being knights in his garden.

Another of the boys was called Arthur. His mother worked in the same factory my father did. He and his mother also attended the same church as us. I therefore saw him on Sundays in the Sunday school class. I think it was more through Sunday school rather than school that I got to know him. Unlike me he had a keen interest in sport and played football in the playground. This put a social divide between us, but on Sunday that division was not there. It was because of the Sunday school connection that I socialised with him and sometimes went to his house which was only a couple of streets away from ours. Our assigned Sunday school teacher was younger than the others and he was called John. I think that Arthur and I got along with John because he was young and a man; a good role model for boys. He was also very intelligent. I cannot say that at this point I loved Sunday school, but I did like John. He was good to talk to.

After Sunday school, Arthur and I would walk home together. On the way we would stop at a sweet shop to buy soft drinks and drink them there. It was a good excuse to spend time talking to the shop owner, Mrs Reddie. I enjoyed this social interaction. I do not think that Arthur and I ever actually talked about Sunday school. It was just something our parents took us to so we put up with it. I did not find it thrilling. We just enjoyed being friends.

Then there was Douglas. At the end of each school day, I would walk to the bus stop with him. He lived in a house diagonally opposite ours at the Road Island that was on the corner of our street. I would tell him stories that I had read in comics. He seemed to enjoy it so I did this every night. I could remember every detail of comics I had read the previous week. In retrospect it was good practice for later remembering scripts for plays.

There was a boy in the class who seemed to have difficulty. His name was Gray. For reasons I cannot understand he frequently got into trouble. He was not a bully, but somehow he got into fights with great regularity and when it happened all the other pupils, including me, would gather round to watch in the knowledge that very soon a teacher would come out to put a stop to it. There was one teacher called Mr Mathews, who was the head teacher. (This was not the same as the headmaster.) Mr Mathews taught primary seven, but he also had the title of head teacher, and he shared disciplinary matters with the headmaster. It was usually Mr Mathews who came out to stop the fights, and we all knew that Gray would face the consequences of his action and suffer corporal punishment. All teachers had a strap of leather that they would use. A pupil caught misbehaving would hold out both hands, one on top of the other, palms up, and the teacher would hit them with the strap. Gray got the strap, which we called 'the belt', far more often than anyone else. Looking back, I can see that Gray did not make any friends. I had only had six months of failing to make friends at my previous school; Gray had seven years of it. I think no one would befriend him because we could see that we would get into a fight and be punished along with him.

Mr Mathews became our teacher in the final year. On that first morning I wondered what it would be like for Gray. He had been sent to Mr Mathews many times to be punished. What would it be like now that we had Mr Mathews as our teacher and he would be spending all day with him? We entered Mr Mathews' classroom and before we sat down, I heard him say, "You! Professor, I have a special desk for you." He looked at Gray and indicated a desk that he had put near his own. It was obvious that Mr Mathews had put it there so that he could watch Gray all the time. It was probably the best thing that could have happened to him because Gray got through the whole year without getting into trouble.

Along the road from the school was the local theatre where once a year we were taken to see six sketches performed. There was a lady who would introduce each sketch. With curtain closed she would make a long cooing noise and then stick her head out to introduce the next one. She would then go off the stage, the curtains would open and the sketch would begin. The format remained the same every year. I developed a love of theatre.

Each year there was a gala. It was another day where normal school life was suspended and we did something very different. The shops in the town were full of Union Jack flags which parents bought for their children. My family always started the gala day by getting my brother and me dressed in our best clothes and well-greased hair to stand on the step outside our house with our flags; there we would be photographed, usually with our grandfather or Aunt Margaret. We would then set off for school. In our imaginations the flags became swords and boys would sword-fence each other in the playground. The time would then come for all of us to leave the school in an orderly fashion to march in a parade with other schools from other parts of the town, carrying our flags to the local park. Each school marched behind their own banner and bands played marching tunes. Our thoughts would be of the summer holidays that would soon come, and we would chant, "Hip hip hooray, this is the gala day; if we don't get a holiday, we'll all run away!" People out doing their shopping, or who had come into town to see the parade, would line the streets to watch. I would try to spot my mother in the crowd as I marched down the High Street.

We marched to the park and entered the gates. There we played games with the teachers. I think that by playing those games each year we started to see our teachers as real people; people who enjoyed having some fun with us for just one day in the year. At the appropriate time our teacher would then distribute white boxes.

The boxes contained our lunch which the school had purchased for us. Sharing this simple meal with my classmates and with the teacher was great fun. After lunch, games would resume for the afternoon. Many parents would come into the park at the end of the day to meet their children and walk home with them. Other children would walk home alone or with friends. I was among the latter. The gala was a highlight of the school year; a day to spend just playing games and having no lessons.

All teachers start out as students, and the day comes when they are thrown to the wolves, meaning, they have to teach while still students for the first time. A student called Miss Dixon came to the school, and she spent the day teaching our class. We boys thought that she was very good looking. She had long blonde hair, lovely eyes and a short skirt. We thought she looked like a model. During break time I was with two friends. The three of us went around the playground with our arms slung over each other's shoulders chanting, "We've got a bird, we've got a bird," so the whole school knew how good looking we thought she was. I saw Miss Dixon one day working in the Co-op Pharmacy so she must have worked there on Saturdays to make some extra money. She showed no sign of recognising me. Doris, who had been our next door neighbour at our previous house, also worked in the pharmacy. I recognised her but said nothing.

Every day, crates of milk were delivered to the school. Each bottle contained one third of a pint and time was set aside for us to drink it. My parents told me that when they were children, milk was delivered to both primary and secondary schools. When I was a child, it was only delivered to primary schools. I loved milk, and from time to time if there had been a miscalculation and there was an extra bottle, I always volunteered to drink it.

Nurse Hood was a district nurse who came to the school and carried out examinations on every child. She checked our hair for head lice, which we called 'nits'. To the best of my knowledge she never found any. She wore a white coat and a dark blue hat that was bowl-shaped – almost like a bowler hat – and white gloves. We would stand in a line in front of her and one by one she would check our ears and our hair with an almost military style. The school did not have a clinic, so this procedure took place in corridors. I think this annual inspection was left over from previous generations when health issues were a much greater concern. The daily milk gave us calcium for strong bones and avoided the problem of rickets. Some of our favourite stories about pirates would feature a character called Bandy. The bow legs were a result of rickets and as this was still in the books and plays for children, this health problem was not far in the past, but in my time nobody in school suffered from this. Nurse Hood recommended and used Kirby combs; these were small combs designed to remove tiny insects from children's hair. By putting it through our hair, any problems would be spotted immediately and parents often also kept these combs. With the examination over and no problems found, we went straight back to the classroom.

Every teacher had a cupboard in which books were kept that the children could borrow and read at leisure. It was in this way that I discovered the Biggles books written by Captain W E Johns. I loved them so much that on one occasion when I got a voucher on Prize-giving Sunday at church, I used it to get an omnibus edition of some of these books. I thought that they were wonderful adventure stories set in the First World War, and when I read that W E Johns was actually a pilot, in my young mind he became Biggles himself, the famous character from my storybooks. From time to time the teacher would ask us to read out loud from these books to the class and recommend them to each other. I must have done this really well because one boy approached me about getting a Biggles book before I had finished reading it.

All primary school teachers taught Gym. In some schools this was called Physical Education. The school did not have a proper gymnasium with wall bars but we did have benches, bean bags, skittles and skipping ropes. Often these lessons would begin with running on the spot. Our teacher, Miss Jackson, told us that we were going to get another teacher for Gym. Her name was Miss Hardy and she warned us that Miss Hardy was very strict. My heart sank at this news. How terrible was Miss Hardy going to be? Would she shout at me? Miss Hardy was a professional Gym teacher. She was an older lady and it was true that she *was* strict. However, this meant that as we had been warned, none of us misbehaved. I found that far from being afraid of her, I loved her lessons. She would put on music and teach us how to dance to it. She stood in front of the class with the music on and proceeded to demonstrate, and we had to copy her moves. She never actually called it dancing. If she had, I think boys would have thought it 'sissy'. She just expected us to copy her, which we obediently did. It was fun. I could see that Miss Hardy enjoyed her job as she smiled at the class while she continued to lead us. As long as we behaved, we had nothing to fear. I found Gym lessons from her to be better than those of our own teacher and much more enjoyable. I loved both the music and the dancing and looked forward to Miss Hardy's visits.

The school was not far from Dunfermline Abbey. One day, to help us with our history lessons, the teacher took us there. Robert the Bruce was buried under the pulpit, which stands on four legs. There is a large brass plaque over the grave with his image carved on it. A man told us that the body had been discovered and re-buried where it now was. He added that before being re-buried, the skeleton had been measured and he had been found to be six feet two inches. The man said that this made him the tallest king that Scotland had ever had. I thought that the Bruce must have seemed like a giant to the people of his day as they were smaller than most modern people and six feet two inches would still be considered very tall today.

The zigzag designs on two of the pillars in the knave cause an optical illusion, which the man demonstrated as he took us round them, telling us to look at them from different angles. From one direction they look thicker at the top than they do at the bottom, but from another direction they appear to be the opposite. He showed us the grave of Queen Margaret in the abbey grounds. She was married to Malcolm Canmore, King of Scotland, and was very popular with the public. He and Margaret lived in a tower a short walk from the abbey and palace. The visit to the abbey gave us an understanding of Dunfermline's history. It was once the capital of

Scotland and the palace ruins are next to the abbey. It filled me with a sense of wonder and pride at this place where I was born and where I lived.

5

The End of an Era

We were living in a time of change. For many years cars crossing the River Forth had to either go by a long route to Kincardine, crossing the river by using the Kincardine Bridge, or go on a ferry. The only other means of crossing was by train on the 19th century Forth Rail Bridge. A road bridge was now built that would put an end to the ferry service. Perhaps my father was feeling nostalgic for the things of the past, or perhaps he just desired to spend some time with me, but he decided that he wanted to be on the last ferry to cross the river and he took me with him. I had never been on a ship before. As we sailed across, I looked at the railway bridge and the new road bridge. I marvelled at how they were constructed. They seemed so strong and majestic. The railway bridge had been the first steel bridge in the world to be built. I enjoyed the trip across the River Forth very much and look back upon it as a unique moment in Scottish history.

A Christian service was conducted on the ship as we crossed, and we sang hymns. I expect that the only other time that that was likely to have happened was when the first ferry had gone across. I realised that I was witnessing something unique. This event would never happen again and I was there to see it.

Going to secondary school in the late 1960s was a big change for me. It was much larger than my primary school and a whole new experience. In the morning I put on my new uniform. I had never worn long trousers before. My brother looked at me and burst into tears. Our mother comforted him as did our Aunt Margaret. Being four years younger than I, it was his first time going to school without me and the thought of going to school alone was probably a bit too much for him.

I left the house and saw some of the other children in our street walking to our new school, so I walked with them. When we got there, we entered the enormous building and sat in the assembly hall. A woman wearing a black teacher's robe read out our names, and as she did so we were to leave the hall following another teacher as indicated. These teachers were to be our register teachers. My class followed a man in a robe just like that of the ladies to one of the science labs. He introduced himself as Mr Keir and he taught Chemistry and Physics. He took the register and then handed out sheets with blank timetables on them. He showed us on his board what to write on the timetable, and in this way we entered all our subjects, school rooms and times for every day of the week. The bell went and we had to find our way to our first lesson along the maze of corridors. We were given two weeks to learn our way around the building. After that, if we were late for lessons we would be punished. We had to walk on the left to prevent congestion. It was inevitable that some of us would get lost.

The morning came to an end, and it was time for dinner. I had a period of technical drawing before dinner and another one after. The teacher told us not to be late coming back. I had to go home to eat, but in the process of trying to find an exit, I got lost. I saw Mr Keir and asked him for the way out. I then went home, had dinner and came back to school – but I was late for the lesson as I got lost in the corridors again. This gave me more motivation to find my way round the building.

I quickly made friends. I also made enemies who bullied me for the next three years. It was friends who made it bearable. Being put back six months at primary school counted against me. I found that my class was in a non-certificate stream, meaning that we would never be presented to sit 'O' levels. The education system had decided that I was a useless 'dunderhead'. We did not discuss this situation with each other, but we all had the same fear. We were afraid of what our future lives would be like without academic qualifications. One boy asked a teacher if we could get good jobs without qualifications. There was a stunned silence. This was the unmentionable question, and we were all thinking it. The teacher was on the spot. Somehow he blurted out, "Yes," and then bluffed his way through an answer.

I was not brilliant, but I knew that I was not a 'dunderhead'. I did not feel that I had done anything to deserve being in that situation. I also believed that I did my work reasonably well but that there was no hope for me. The thought of being turfed out of school with no qualifications felt like a looming deadly monster coming for me – and there was nothing I could do to stop it. All I could do was get on with my work and enjoy school until that day came.

In a large school, it is important to have a strong man at the top. The headmaster was such a character. We nicknamed him Boris after the actor Boris Karloff who played the Frankenstein monster in the films. Boris used morning assembly to get some points over to us. He told us exactly what he thought of bad behaviour and what the consequences would be. There were many occasions when, in exasperation, a teacher or prefect would send a boy – it was usually boys – to him to be belted for their persistent bad behaviour. I was not one of those boys, but I knew those who were, as they were the ones who bullied me, and I thought they deserved what they got. It was in one such assembly that Boris told us that when he called in parents because of their child's bad behaviour, he often found that the child's attitude was a reflection of what the parents were like. He also found that when a child who thought he was a 'big man' was in his office to be belted, he was not so big then.

Some incidents of bad behaviour were major. The school had an intake from a vast area, so some pupils had to come by bus. The boys from one particular village would sometimes take out the light bulbs on the upper deck and throw them out the windows. They also lifted the cushions from the seats and threw them around. Boris was furious. He told us that he had had enough and that from now on he would no longer deal with the situation. If it happened again then the bus company would have to call the police and charge them. It never happened again. Such was the fear we had of Boris.

Boris had been a teacher during the Second World War, and often told us of his boys who had not come home. As a mark of respect for them, sometimes at assembly the school band would play the tune 'The Dam Busters'. Many years later, I found that one of my Maths teachers had been one of his boys who *had* come home.

Boris had a very distinctive voice. The sound of it, as we walked in the corridors between classes, telling us to get into single file on the left, filled us with dread. He was a tall, stalky man with a bald head and blue eyes. On one occasion in my first year, my English teacher was off ill and Boris took the class. To my surprise, I really enjoyed the lesson. Boris was an amazing teacher. I think English must have been his own subject when he was a classroom teacher because he seemed to have such a mastery of it. He was able to take up from where our teacher had left off yet he had not prepared for it. He knew his subject very well indeed.

As one moved up the school years, one met people one had not seen in previous years as they were the sons and daughters of people who had moved into the area. They would seem to materialise out of nowhere. One such boy was Dennis. It was because of him that I saw what would prove to be my first observation of what culture shock was like. Although Dennis was British, he had grown up in Rhodesia. Every day in conversation he would mention Rhodesia this, Rhodesia that. We found it very annoying. He missed the place that he called home

There were no black faces in the school but Dennis seemed to think that he could make whatever remarks he wanted to about black people without impunity. All of us got annoyed at him as we thought that he looked down on anyone whose skin colour did not reflect his own. For us, these black people were purely imaginary, but for him they were real. They were people he had known. I tried to befriend him as did my other friends, but we could not agree with the views that he held to. He had just arrived in the country and knew no better. He must have felt like a fish out of water. In our minds there was an assumption that all students were local, or came from other parts of the East of Scotland. We were totally unprepared for Dennis. He stayed for about a year. I have no idea if his family moved on, or if they decided that it was all a bit too much for their son, but I never saw him again. However, I now look back and draw lessons from those days. I had not realised at the time how strongly influenced by my local culture I was and that my point of view was not the only point of view. Life was not as simple as I wanted it to be. Dennis had a vastly different worldview to anyone else at the school. He had been one of the ruling minority but had now come to a new environment where he was the underdog and where we put him down every time that he said something we did not agree with. It must have been very lonely for him.

6

The Question Must Be Answered

One day stands out in my mind, on which something happened that eventually led to changing my life. We were all told to go to the assembly hall. It was on a day that we did not normally go to assembly, so I knew that something out-of-the-ordinary was going to happen. When we went in, there were little books on the chairs. I picked one up and sat down. I had a look at it and could see that it was the New Testament.

Boring!

There were two men on the stage whom I had never seen before. They told us that they were from the Gideons society and that they put New Testaments in schools and hotels. One of the men then directed us to the copies we had found on our seats and said, "We trust you will read them."

"There is no chance of that," I thought. "I have tried reading the Bible; it is boring."

I took it home and put it on my bookshelf, where it stayed for about a year. Some boys tore pages out or theirs, others made inky marks. I ignored mine completely. It just stayed gathering dust on the shelf. I was determined not to read it.

One night, I had difficulty getting to sleep. I sat up and looked at my books, and my eye fell on that New Testament. So I picked it up and began to read it. It was full of genealogies which were not all that interesting. However, in my mind I set myself a challenge. I decided to read a chapter every night just to prove to myself that I could do it. One night I reached the end of John's gospel and I read these words: "This is the disciple who testifies to these things and who wrote them down. We know that his testimony is true. Jesus did many other things as well. If every one of them were written down, I suppose that even the whole world would not have room for the books that would be written."[2]

This struck at my heart and I was deeply moved by it. Here was a man who had written this and who had seen Jesus. He had heard what Jesus had said, he had seen him perform miracles, die and come back from the dead, and in those verses he was claiming that he knew it was all true because he had personally seen it. This made me take the Bible very seriously. I had dismissed it up to that point, but I could not ignore this new feeling I had of wanting to read it more and more and to find out what it had to say. Somehow I knew that Jesus had died for sin and risen again and that he was some sort of saviour, but I really did not have a clear idea of what that meant.

At school, I was the elephant in the room. I was reasonably intelligent but in a non-certificate stream, and just like the emperor's new clothes, it sometimes takes just one person to say it and then everybody else agrees. For me, that person was a new teacher who came from Boston in the USA. He was called Mr Moss and he taught English.

One day he said, "Mr Falconer, you should not be in this class." I already knew that, but I had never heard anyone else say it. He went on to say, "I am going to speak to one of my colleagues and see if you can be transferred to his class."

He was as good as his word and I was put in another English class that was in a certificate stream. There was some hope for me at last.

---

[2] John 21:24-25

I started in the new class that entitled me to sit 'O' level English. This was a great encouragement to me and I did pass. I wanted to stay on at school beyond the age of fifteen, but my parents were told in a meeting with Boris that this would not be possible. However, there was a second meeting. I have no idea what was said but I think that my success at English may have played a part in it. I did stay on and repeated 'third year'. This opened the way to other subjects and on to 'Highers'.

I loved my senior years. Those who bullied me left school; I made new friends and life was good. I took part in the school operetta. I loved the theatre and music, and this cultivated my love of it. We performed in the local theatre, the same one that I had seen the sketches performed in when I was at primary school. In the process of taking part, I got to know other students. The Music, English and Art departments worked together to put the production on.

The cast became the school choir and sometimes we were asked to sing outside of the normal school environment. One day I came home at lunchtime from school. My father opened the door and told me that my grandfather had died that day. The choir were to sing at a local dance hall that night. I participated in it as though nothing had happened. I found coping with my grandfather's death difficult and did not go the funeral, but stayed at home with my brother. It was my first experience of the death of a loved one that I could remember.

I decided to participate in a second operetta that the school put on. Rehearsals started but I had to drop out due to illness. I had a pain that turned out to be appendicitis. I had the operation and was absent from school for a short time at the start of my final year.

When I was in hospital there were two other men in the room with me. Both were considerably older then I was. We got talking about spiritual things. One man was called Ted. He said, "Jesus Christ was either the biggest colossal liar who ever existed or he told the simple truth."

The other added, "Only believe. That is what Jesus said. Only believe."

Over the years I have come to value that conversation and those words. You either accept Jesus or you do not. There is nothing in between.

One day, after returning to school, I saw a very attractive girl in the library, whom I had never seen before. I could not take my eyes off her; she was absolutely gorgeous. Moreover, I later discovered that she was in my Art class. I could not have been more pleased to see her! Amy's family had recently moved to the town, and she was the daughter of an actor I greatly admired. One day Mr Ross, our new Art teacher, took us to a gallery in Edinburgh. He had a minibus to take us and when I arrived I found that there was only one seat left; it was beside Amy. I really enjoyed Edinburgh that day. It was the first time Amy and I spoke. She wanted to know what subjects I was interested in. Evidently she had also spotted me. We became good friends and I loved Art lessons all the more because of her company. I looked forward to seeing her every day.

I considered my own painting skills to be average, but I thought she excelled at it. I think she also found me just as attractive, but I was too shy to ask her out. I loved the fact that she appreciated me even though I was so shy. I loved watching her paint, and sometimes she would watch me do likewise. I was still affected by those verses I had read in John's gospel; a lot of the paintings I did in the Art class that year were on Bible themes.

Mr Ross implied that my interest in spiritual matters was just a phase I was going through, but I knew he was wrong. Something deep had happened within me and it would not pass away. I determined in my heart that one day I would prove that to him.

The final school year was different from any other year. The school was the smallest it had ever been in its history; there were just two hundred of us. Assembly was even smaller and Boris did not stand on the stage. He put a chair on the floor in front of us, sat on it and talked to us in such a fashion that it was clear that he expected us to keep the junior school under control. We were also given more responsibility. The school had a programme called Community Service. There were options to choose from and it was aimed at the elderly. Girls could go to an elderly person's home to chat to them and perhaps help with light duties. The boys had two options. We could either do gardening or we could go to visit the elderly infirm in a nearby hospital.

As I had no interest in gardening, I chose to go to the hospital. It had previously been a poor house or workhouse, and among many of the population it still had that shameful reputation even though it had long ceased to have that function. There were two men's wards and a ladies' ward. As a boy, I was only permitted to go to the men's wards. I found that some of them never had a visitor from the start to the finish of any week. This made me the only visitor, and I was young and a complete stranger to them. Most of them were almost bedridden.

One man was blind. His name was David. He lay in bed with his cap on. To anyone who said hello, he always asked the same question: "Are you saved?" David was a member of the Brethren Church and one of my teachers was in the same assembly. I saw him and another man visit David several times. He loved to have the Bible read to him. I think the loss of his sight must have been a terrible blow to him as he could no longer read it for himself, but he clearly loved it. When it was read he would take off his cap as a mark of respect for what God had to say. I wonder how many people became followers of Jesus as a result of that old man asking the question, "Are you saved?" I expect that for many it was an uncomfortable question to be asked, but it had to be answered.

7

An Unexpected Change

The church my family attended was in financial difficulty and merged with another church. I found this upsetting. It had been a regular fixture in my life, and some of the people in it were family friends whom I had known all my life. Change can be difficult, and this was a change that I had not expected and was not prepared for. I felt out of control. I thought that the new minister was old and boring, and I had had enough of being bored in church. I did not say that to my parents for fear of starting an argument; instead, I told them I would find another church.

I planned to go round visiting all the churches I could. I was sure I would find all of them boring and then drop out, and my parents would find that so awful that they would just let me go my own way and I would never be in church again.

The Sunday came when I planned to visit the first church. On that day, I said to God, "If I am ever going to go to this place a second time, I am going to have to be awfully impressed with the preaching, and as I have never heard impressive preaching, that is not likely to happen, is it?" – and off I went.

I met a couple of the boys from school at the church, and one of the girls. "At least I will get to talk to them," I thought.

On arrival there were no hymn books left. I went up on the balcony and a lady and her daughter noticed that I did not have one. The lady gave me hers and shared her daughter's. I found that little gesture very moving.

Soon the time came for the sermon. I prepared to be bored but, to my surprise, I found it gripping. The minister directly applied what he said to himself. I had never heard anything like it. As I came down the stairs to leave, I said in my heart, "OK God, I must admit, that was impressive."

When I got to the door, the minister stopped me and introduced me to Kate, a girl a few years older than me, and to a couple called Thomson. I enjoyed talking to them. The man was one of the elders. And so I changed my mind: I decided to go back.

My second visit resulted in me being invited by Kate to the youth fellowship. I went and met other people of my own age. I also met the president of the youth fellowship. He was an Englishman called Bob, and I already knew him because he was a teacher at my school. I went a third time, then a fourth – and six months went by.

Kate became like an older sister to me. One Sunday evening she asked me, "Do you think you will settle in your new church?" I had not said anything to her about church. Perhaps she had perceived that I had had no intention of staying on that first day I had met her. It was she, the family and the impressive preaching that had made me want to stay, and after six months I had no intention of leaving.

Bob invited me to the Scripture Union he and two other teachers had started at school. I spent all of my final year attending those meetings. Sometimes we would have a sing-along at lunchtime and invite other students to it. Bob would lead us with his guitar. He loved singing.

I had a double life with Bob. One life was at church where he was a young man in his late twenties who was President of the youth fellowship; the other was at school where I had to address him in a manner suitable for a teacher. This made me feel so privileged to have such a friend. The other boys at the church were in the same situation with him. Looking back, I expect it was difficult for Bob, but I respected him and the people around him for their faithfulness to God and their integrity.

Every New Year, or Hogmanay as it is known in Scotland, the minister and his wife would have a party at their house, to which Bob and I, along with other members of the youth fellowship, were invited, as well as some other members of the congregation. For me these parties were the highlight of the year. I was spending time with a group of people I had grown to dearly love. There were two brothers in the fellowship, Ian and Eric. Ian had a keen interest in photography and by using a projector, he would let us see slide photographs of the church that he had taken that year. It was like looking back over our lives for the past twelve months and remembering the good times we had had. We were so appreciative of one another and to Ian for taking the pictures. I thought these photographs were a good record of the life of the church. They seemed to tell my story and the stories of the people around me.

I felt close to Bob at the time and to the others in the youth fellowship. Having met the Thomsons on my first visit to the church, I got to know their three children: Bethany, Patricia and Graham.

Bethany was the oldest child. She was a very intelligent girl who went to university. We were given the sad news that she had somehow passed out and fallen from a balcony and had sustained serious injuries. She was only eighteen years old but she was put on a life support machine. Time passed by and we could see the look of anguish every time we saw her parents, brother and sister. We prayed for the family, for we felt their grief. Sometimes, however, God does not give us what we ask for, and I expect that her parents asked that she would be restored. She was not. One day her parents made the decision that must have been so hard for them. They gave permission to have the machine switched off. There was no brain activity, she was clinically dead, and the family accepted that she was with the Lord.

I cannot begin to understand what they, as parents, or her brother and sister went through, or what they still go through. Perhaps as the years went by they wondered what she would have been doing now if she were still with them. God, however, had taken her to be with him. The family's faith stood this test. They were still loyal to the Lord. They were like Job who was able to say while he was suffering, "Though he slay me, yet will I hope in him; I will surely defend my ways to his face."[3] They never gave up!

The parents are now also with the Lord, but as I was Bethany's age at the time, this event had a profound effect on me. It affected the whole church. It re-emphasises that if we hear the Lord calling us to repentance and faith, then *now* is the time to do it. One should not put it off, for we never know when we may suddenly be snatched from this life to appear before God to be judged.

I felt a lump in my throat at one meeting where, once again, Ian was showing photos, but not only of the past year. He had put together as many photos of the church as he was able to find. As we looked at the pictures and saw ourselves in them, someone asked, "Who is that?" and pointed out a young lady who had broken the heel off her shoe and was sitting on a rock holding it. Mrs Thomson spoke up, and I could almost hear the tears in her voice as she said, "It is Bethany." My mind went back to the day that the photo was taken. We had all gone out for a long walk and Bethany's high heels had not been really very appropriate for walking in the countryside. Suddenly one of her heels broke. She sat down, took off her shoe and held up the heel. We all smiled and laughed. What had been an unexpected and humorous moment captured on camera was now a timely reminder to us of the young woman we had all loved and lost.

---

[3] Job 13:15

8

Good with Food

I was not as successful at getting qualifications at school as I would have like to have been but I left with a few, which was considerably more than I had expected when I first went there. Most of my classmates who started with me left with nothing. I had no idea what I wanted to do with my life. I had no job.

Then I managed to get employment in the Co-operative Society in the main supermarket as a storeman. I knew a few of the staff as they had been at school with me. I also knew the manager, Mr McPhilips, because he had once managed the Co-op near our house, and he was a lay preacher who had sometimes preached in my first church before it had closed. I looked up to Mr McPhilips. I was told by some of the staff that one of his friends came into the shop every week and it was known that he was a shoplifter. The man was pointed out to me and I had to follow him. I did this often, and one day the man confronted me and accused me of following him, which indeed I was. Somehow Mr McPhilips found out about this and he said, "Do you know that man comes to my house?" He comforted me and said, "I always support my staff." Evidently he knew that his friend was a thief and had told the rest of the staff that if he were ever caught it would be better to take him to the assistant manager. I realised that although Mr McPhilips was in a difficult position, he was determined to do the right thing. I saw him as a man of integrity and I respected that. He was a good example of what a Christian man ought to be.

As I already knew some people in the shop, the change from school to being a working man was relatively easy for me. I loved the work Mondays to Wednesdays, but less so Thursdays to Saturdays as I spent those days gathering customer shopping trollies and baskets, filling their bags, or packing their purchases into boxes to be delivered to their homes; I did not find this very interesting at all. It did, however, encourage me to talk to the ladies on the tills or those who were filling the shelves, and I got to know some of the regular customers. In this way, I learned some people skills.

I knew that I did not want to spend the rest of my life in a shop; but in the meantime it was job. I loved the people I worked with, and from time to time, for staff relief, I would be sent to other shops. I enjoyed that for meeting other people in these shops; some of them had been on the staff of the same branch I worked in and it was good to see them again.

On one occasion I was sent out to a shop where I knew the assistant manager. I had met Davey in my shop when he had been a trainee manager. I was in the office with him when he said, "Come with me." I followed him round the shop wondering what we were doing – because that is all we seemed to be doing: wandering around the shop, just walking and walking, doing nothing.

As we passed by the customers, some of them would talk to him and say, "Hello Davey, how are you doing?"

I thought this was a friendly greeting, but as we continued to walk, Davey said to me, "I have had him for shoplifting." There were in fact several convicted shoplifters in the shop and this was 'squaring up' to them. They were letting Davey know they were there and Davey was acknowledging this, and it felt like being a gunfighter at the OK Corral. Who would blink first?

Later, Davey sent one of the staff to get me for he had caught a shoplifter and he needed a witness as the bags were searched. We did find the goods on the man, but unlike most shoplifters he continued to deny it. This meant that there had to be a trial. Davey and I had to take time out of work to appear for the prosecution. We sat through a number of cases before our one came up. It seemed to me that real life was not like watching Perry Mason, a fictional lawyer on TV who never lost a case and whose cases were very dramatic. The real thing was like watching a factory at work. The prosecuting lawyer would read from his notes and the judge would pass a sentence. Most of it was routine as there was no defence offered in most cases. This was the product of the factory.

I took the stand and although I did my best, and I did remember the case, I could not remember all the fine details. This resulted in a 'not proven' verdict. In Scotland we have three verdicts: 'not guilty', 'guilty' and 'not proven'. This verdict is a polite way of saying that "we are letting you go, but we think you are guilty; we just do not have enough evidence to prove it". This result was disappointing and the shoplifter left court a free man.

As I had not long been out of school, I was not much older than the Saturday girls. A great deal of flirting went on, but on the whole, I think they were a nice bunch – very attractive and good friends to have. I looked forward to seeing them every weekend.

My parents kept fairly good health and I took that for granted. But a day came when we had a shocking reminder of how fragile our lives really are. Our father passed out and fell off a ladder at work, hurting his hand on a glass door. He was kept in hospital for tests and observation.

I had passed my driving test and had my first car, so I drove the family to the hospital to see him. I could not believe this was happening. I saw my father in a hospital bed. He had seemed indestructible. He was one of the longest serving employees in the factory where he worked, and this incident came as a major shock to them.

The managing director saw to it that my parents would have a holiday in Switzerland when my father recovered. My parents had never been abroad together before; as far as I know the only time my father had ever ventured out of the country was during the war when he had been a conscript. They had the holiday and then life returned to normal, but it had shown me that one unexpected incident could suddenly overpower us as a family.

I was to drive the family to the hospital again on a number of occasions, because my brother was often in severe pain. The worrying thing was that we had no idea why. He would go to bed when the pain would start. Eventually the problem was diagnosed and he had an operation. In that situation I found that my parents clung on to the slightest hopeful sign. We were visiting my brother in hospital after the operation and as we all left, my father remarked to my mother that there was colour in my brother's cheeks. It was their way of coping. I had not noticed this colour, but I think my father's observation was correct. I said nothing, for I knew the seriousness of the situation and I was looking for bigger signs of improvement, such as his strength returning and being permanently free of the pain. I would never notice a bit of colour in his cheeks, but I suppose parents have a different way of looking at things. My brother went on to make a good recovery.

9

God's Gift to Mankind

Like most young men of the time, I enjoyed popular music. Every Thursday night I was in front of the television watching Top of the Pops to see which song was number one in the charts. I also loved listening to The Breakfast Show on Radio One and playing my records.

There was a musical event in our local theatre. A Christian singing group had come from Florida, USA, though I did not know anything about them. It was very different to the sort of music I usually listened to but I enjoyed it. There was one song called Cornerstone in which a male soloist had to hit a very high note at the end. I was astonished that a man could sing so well and actually hit that note.

The next day, my brother Jim and I were in church, where a man was sitting in front of us. Jim said, "You see that man? He was with that group last night. He was not on the stage with them, but he was with them." We realised that it was likely that the man was American, and meeting people from overseas in Dunfermline was very unusual. I decided to stop the man as he was leaving and talk to him. We were right; he *was* American, and he had been with the group.

As we talked, he said his name was Richard. He then spoke about the message that he and the group were spreading. He said that the Bible says, "For the wages of sin is death, but the gift of God is eternal life in Christ Jesus our Lord."[4] He then asked, "What do you do to receive a gift?" Richard held out his hands as though receiving a gift from me. He said, "A gift is not something you earn. A gift is something you receive. It is given to you. All you have to do is receive it." He continued to say that we are all sinners, we all deserve God's wrath, but God through his grace has paid the penalty of our sins and he offers us eternal life. It is a gift, but we have to receive it, and we receive it by trusting in Jesus Christ and his death on the cross in our place.

This conversation was a turning point to me. It was as though I had been in a dark room and suddenly all the lights had come on and I could see for the first time in my life. In that moment I needed to receive the gift and in that moment I was converted. I knew who God was, I knew Jesus was the Son of God, I knew I was a sinner; I knew that I had just accepted and trusted him. The gift of eternal life was mine. My life had just turned around. All those Sunday school stories I knew seemed to come together and make sense.

Richard invited us to a Bible study at his house which he called 'Ranch'. Jim and I went, and there were other young people present. We met his wife, Cindy, and we went to Ranch every week. In these meetings Richard would explain the gospel by using his hands and a wallet. He held one hand up, palm upwards, and said, "Let this hand represent us." He then said, "Let this wallet represent sin." He put the wallet on his hand. "We all have sin on us. The Bible says, '...for all have sinned and fall short of the glory of God.'[5] There is nothing we can do to earn salvation." He then held up his other hand and said, "Let this hand represent God." He took the wallet from the first hand and explained, "God has taken our sin upon himself in Jesus Christ and paid for it on the cross. He has died for us and risen again." Then he would hold up the empty hand that

[4] Romans 6:23
[5] Romans 3:23

represented us and show us the empty palm and say, "Because Christ has paid for our sin, we no longer need to face the penalty of Hell. God has forgiven us, if only we will trust in Christ." I thought this was a good, simple illustration of the gospel message.

Scarlet is the colour of sin, and I realised that my sin, even the so called 'little things' were deep scarlet. When you trust the Lord and are a follower of Jesus as I then was, all those little things become so big and daunting. They need to be dealt with.

Once, when I visited Richard and Cindy, Cindy asked me what I thought repentance was. I said that it was feeling sorry for my sins. But she said that it was more than that; it was a *turning around;* it meant changing my mind or going in a different direction. As she talked, I realised that I had in fact repented and was continuing to do so. Being sorry for sin was a starting point but real repentance means stopping doing the sinful things, out of a desire to please God. I could not earn eternal life by repenting because even if I was perfect from that day on, I still had the problem of all my sin up to that point. I knew Jesus had paid for it all, but what Cindy said to me gave me a much clearer idea of repentance. Most people agree that stealing is a sin. If someone steals and says, "I repent," but makes a habit of stealing, then he has not repented. However, if he stops stealing then he has repented. Repentance starts when we put our trust in Christ to save us from sin. It means that our lives will change. We stop depending on ourselves and depend on him.

As I attended church and Ranch, I started to get to grips with what sin is. It seems like an old-fashioned word that is rarely used, and when it is, we think of it in terms of gross sin, such as murder. However, it is more than that. Sin is our nature. It is in the DNA of all humans. It is even part of the way we think.

Thus it was that I continued attending Ranch meetings, hearing the gospel over and over again and seeing Richard's visual illustration. As time went on, another American couple came to join them called Larry and Kathy. I very quickly grew to love them. Richard was a very sporty individual and had a very athletic type of figure. Larry was the opposite – a quieter man, and Kathy seemed utterly devoted to him. To these two couples I owe a lot. It was they who took us to see a Christian ship. At the time all I knew was that those of us attending Ranch could go and see this ship. I thought that would be an adventure, something exciting, so I went. I remember very little about it except that we all went up the gangway, boarded the ship and were shown round it. It was later that I realised the ship was the Operation Mobilisation (OM) ship 'MV Doulos'. I did not know it at the time, but this was to be my first contact with OM. I think Ranch was good for me, but I never attended Ranch at the expense of attending church.

I learned that when one truly believes and trusts in Jesus, it is such a wonderful thing to find that sin is forgiven, but one also finds out that one is a greater sinner than one realised. The Apostle Paul called himself the chief of sinners. One finds that some things that seemed OK are in fact displeasing and sinful to God. It is therefore important to confess sin to him and, where necessary, to those whom we have sinned against. Some people call this 'keeping short accounts'.

Sometimes I had disagreements with Richard. One of them concerned an evening he wanted to organise. It was a Parents' Night to which all parents would be invited to see what we were doing, and in this way he would make contact with them. For me this smacked of being treated like a child. I was not a schoolboy, I was twenty years old; I thought this was highly inappropriate for someone of my age and I said so. I thought, "Perhaps that is OK in America, but in Scotland we are adults. If he wants to meet my parents, I have no objection, but not in this manner."

The meeting went ahead, but I did not invite my parents. I would have felt demeaned if I had. However, I did appreciate Richard's desire to meet them, so I set this up. When I told him he could meet my parents, his jaw looked like it would drop to the floor with shock! He accepted.

We all met in Larry and Kathy's house for dinner. During that time, Larry asked the question, "If you died today, where do you think you would you go? Are you going to heaven?"

Mum seemed uncomfortable.

After a short silence, Dad said, "I am going to heaven." He then related an experience he had had meeting an evangelist who had explained the gospel to him during the Second World War. Dad would have been a conscript at the time. I had never heard Dad say this before and I was amazed!

Richard never had a Parents' Night again!

10

The Engine Room

On a ship the engine room is where the power is. There is a dark gloom about engine rooms. They have no natural light and so white lights are necessary for the engineers to see. I was to find that prayer meetings are like engine rooms. They are where the power of God is enacted and the people at the meetings are like the engineers.

In church every Sunday there were what was called 'Intimations'. This meant that events for the coming week were announced. Each week a prayer meeting was announced, but I had never been to one before. I was curious to know what it would be like, but I lacked the courage to go on my own. Someone had to invite me. Evidently God knew this, as in his providence he gave me a reason to go. One Sunday as I was going into church there were two old ladies walking in front of me. One of them turned round, smiled and greeted me, and in the course of the conversation that followed, she invited me to the prayer meeting. This was the very invitation I needed. The lady was Mrs Whiteford and I wonder if she could have imagined what a big change her kind invitation would make on my life. Attendance at such meetings has become a lifelong habit and she was the first person who set me that example. Some people influence others just by the lives they lead and the things they say. Mrs Whiteford was such a person. I accepted her invitation and went to the prayer meeting at the first opportunity.

The meeting was in the manse. There was some teaching from the Bible led by the minister, and then there was discussion about what we should pray for. Having mentioned things for prayer, everyone in the meeting got down to the business of praying. I could see that there were people there whom I already knew. I also discovered over time that if you want to get to know a church, you do that at the prayer meeting. It is usually there that you find the real church. They are people who believe the Bible and you can see it in their lives. They do not just talk about it, they put it into practice. I discovered that many people who attend the prayer meetings are not those who are the most vocal or have prominent personalities; they are, however, the most faithful and loving.

I had thought that prayer was a formal thing. I had been brought up reciting a prayer that went something like this: "This night as I lie down to sleep, I pray the Lord my soul to keep. If I should die before I wake, take me to heaven for Jesus' sake. Please bless Mummy and Daddy. Please bless Auntie Margaret and Grandad. Help Auntie Margaret to get better. Please bless Auntie Chrissie, Uncle Tommy, Iain and Jim."

Learning to pray is good but this was just recital. I found at the prayer meeting that people never recited pre-written prayers. They spoke to God about the things they cared about and they used their own words. This was a good lesson for me. I realised that I had to do likewise. After a few weeks of attending the prayer meeting, I decided to have a go at it. I would pray out loud without any prepared words and I would take up the same issues that everyone else in the meeting prayed about. It felt glorious. I loved the prayer meeting.

We prayed for ourselves, but we also looked outside of our church asking God to bless the ministries of other men around Scotland. I think that we saw those prayers being answered at the time, for there were many godly ministers who focussed on preaching from the Bible and were not involved in the common activities of jumble sales, sales of work, and various social and fundraising activities. They were more interested in getting people to understand what God has to say to mankind in the Bible. I found that I profited from this greatly in my own life.

Prayer is the act of talking to God. When we talk to God, the act of prayer is not magic. Prayer in itself is just words. The power is in the one prayed to. It is therefore essential that we know God as the person he is. When I started praying in those church meetings, I knew God a little. But I discovered that I got to know God a lot better by praying. He alone answers prayer. I also discovered that God is not like a genie in the tales of the Arabian knights who grants wishes. God answers prayer in accordance with his will and how it glorifies the Father. From our perspective there seems to be some prayer that is not answered, but I believe there is no such thing as unanswered prayer. There are answers to prayer that are unexpected and surprising, there are times when the answer to prayer is no, and there are other times when we ask amiss and it is only for our consumption and not the glory of our heavenly Father, and to that he says no. I do not believe, however, that God ignores prayer. The Bible teaches, "And I will do whatever you ask in my name, so that the Father may be glorified in the Son. You may ask me for anything in my name, and I will do it."[6]

The prayer meeting was by far the best place for fellowship, yet as one visiting speaker put it, "The Prayer meeting is the Cinderella of the church." He meant that considering the size of the congregation, attendance at the prayer meeting was small, and this was by no means unique to my church; it was common across the churches. One has to ask the question, would God do more if more people were at the prayer meeting? I do not know, but I do know that God wants us to pray. The Bible warns that "you do not have because you do not ask"[7].

People of every age were at the prayer meeting. There was Doris, who had lived with her mother next to our house when I was a small child, and whom I had later seen working at the pharmacy.

---

[6] John 14:13-14
[7] James 4:2

It was good to meet her again. I had recognised her as soon as I had seen her in the church. There was also Kate, whom I had met on my first day; she was among the youngest. And there were several retired people, including widows.

11

Upon This Rock

Ranch was good for spending time with people of my age. At church I had the youth fellowship and I was learning about God at a great speed. I was excited and I needed more. I had a car and I would go out to one of the villages to pick up a girl who attended Ranch. As we drove we would make small talk. I had met her at school and she was a few years below me. There was a lot of competition among the boys for the affections of the girls.

As Ranch grew, Richard moved the meetings into his garage. Ranch gave me focus and drive, but church gave me stability.

On one occasion I discovered that there was a meeting being led by a Church of Scotland minister in the next town and what this man had to say would be very interesting. I attended this meeting and most of what he had to say was about how he had come to be a Christian. The thing that he heavily emphasised was that he had been appointed as an elder in the Church of Scotland for ten years before he finally heard and understood the gospel and became a true believer. He had a deep concern for those like himself who had been deceived into thinking they were believers who were right with God because they did good things and were members of the church, but were in fact enemies of God because of their unbelief.

On the day I had stood with two others in front of the church making certain public promises, I joined the organisation we call church; but it was on the day I was converted, when talking to Richard, that I had become a member of the real church. We are taught that we attend church to worship God, but I do not find in the scriptures any of the apostles making such a claim. They gathered for prayer, teaching and fellowship and to encourage one another. It is this that is the function of the church for the believer. If we are true believers, we are called to worship God all the time with every breath of our bodies and with everything we think and do.

Right from the start, I loved the prayer meeting. It was one of the highlights of the week. I realised that even when it was less than inspiring, prayer was vital work. God had commanded us to pray and so prayer was at least an act of obedience to him and, I now realised, was part of the work of the church. It was usually the case on the Sunday morning that people would gather and then, at the end of the service, go straight home, with little or no time for fellowship. The prayer meeting was very different. People always lingered to talk after it. This bonded us together, people of all ages in a common bond of fellowship.

Over the years, we welcomed all sorts of people, including those with personality disorders. In so doing we showed the love of God. It is a disgrace when the church becomes so middle class and worldly that the broken-hearted and unloved cannot find what they need in God's people.

It was also at the prayer and Bible study meetings that I discovered something about myself. One day the minister approached three young men of whom I was one. He asked all three of us to speak on a Bible passage of our choice for ten minutes each at the following week's Bible study. I had never preached before, but we chose a passage and all three of us spoke. From this it was discovered that two of us had the ability to teach, and from that day on there were times when we were asked to preach at the Bible study. Neither of us were asked again to only do it for ten minutes; we were expected to lead the entire evening and the minister would be present as he appreciated being ministered to. I found that I loved preaching. The very thing I had once thought boring was a gift that God had given to me, and I loved it. I had the responsibility of using the gift well and the minister encouraged me in it.

I am struck by the following Bible passage: "Not many of you should become teachers, my fellow believers, because you know that we who teach will be judged more strictly."[8] From this, I conclude that teaching is no light thing. God has charged us with more responsibility in influencing others and he expects us to do it correctly. I have also reached the conclusion that God gives the gift of teaching therefore we have no choice. If we have such a gift then God expects us to use it; not only will he judge us if we do it badly but he will judge us severely if we avoid doing it.

Ranch inspired me to do things to reach those who as yet did not trust in Jesus Christ. To that end I obtained leaflets that I thought were good at communicating the gospel and I gave them to as many people as I could. I also thought that there were many people just like me who enjoyed music and perhaps music could be used to bring people together to listen to what I had to say. So my brother and I learned how to play the guitar. Jim taught himself to play base and I played six string rhythm. We brought two others into the band as they had the musical experience that we lacked. However, one of them very quickly decided not to be involved. The other one was argumentative and arguments occurred frequently. I decided that we needed to drop him and get someone else or we would always be wasting time in pointless arguing. We recruited a friend, Don, whom I knew from school and also from Ranch. He also taught himself how to play the guitar and the three of us became a band.

As we were seeking to proclaim the gospel so that Christ would be revealed to people, it was agreed that we would call ourselves 'Revelation'. All of us sang, and soon we were singing in harmony. I wish I could say we were great, but the truth is that at best we were average. The sound of the band in my head always

---

[8] James 3:1

sounded better than the one I heard in my ears, but at least we were in tune. We attempted to enter a competition and to that end we recorded ourselves and I sent the recording off. The letter of reply I got was polite but it was a rejection. It did not, however, put us off setting up our own concerts, which we did in a variety of churches.

We sang at our own church. One of the girls in our fellowship was sarcastic and clearly did not like the band. I can understand that point of view. However, when I heard the sarcasm, I thought, "Well we may not be that great, but at least we are doing *something.* We are trying to reach out to others and that is what all Christians should be doing."

On one occasion, we played in a working men's club. This was a very different sort of audience, but still not the sort of audience we were aiming at. I envisioned us playing to people our own age. However, we were gaining experience. At every concert, we would take a break in the music to talk to the audience and tell them that we are all sinners and that Jesus had died for our sins and that they too should trust him. To me this address was the whole point of doing these concerts. It was in my opinion more likely that people would respond to what was said rather than the unfamiliar words of a song. I always had something to say from the Bible or from my own experience of walking with God, and prayed that it would make a difference in the lives of the hearers, that some of them at least would repent and believe and be ushered into the kingdom of heaven.

We did one concert in a church in another town. This time it was the sort of audience we were looking for: slightly younger than us and more open to what we were attempting to do. I found that an encouragement. I also decided that I needed a clean cut image and to that end I bought a white suit that I had seen in a shop window and wore it at every performance.

I knew other believers in bands. I knew two who were on the staff of the local Christian bookshop. I approached both of them with a view to putting on a concert in the local theatre. They agreed and we advertised it in all the churches. This was to be our final performance and the highlight of three years playing together. I had attended that theatre in my primary school days, I had been in the school opera in that theatre in my secondary school days, and here I was – a grown man – singing in it to proclaim the gospel to as many people as I could in one night. I hope that some of the things I said in all these concerts took root in people's lives.

I left the Co-op in Dunfermline to take up a new job in another Co-op, this time in Cowdenbeath. There was a greater variety of tasks to be done in my new job. I had never cut meat before, so I learned how to use a meat slicer and keep cooked and cold meat separate to avoid contamination. It also provided me with the opportunity to talk to the staff about Jesus and my relationship with him. I explained how he had come into my life and saved me from sin, and that if they would also believe, he would do the same for them. It gave me some experience talking to people and answering their questions as best as I could.

It was clear that the management thought that they could persuade me to train as a manager, but I still did not want to spend my life in shops.

I was reading the Bible every night. One day, I was reading the Apostle Paul's first letter to Timothy, when I felt deeply moved by the following words: "Don't let anyone look down on you because you are young, but set an example for the believers in speech, in conduct, in love, in faith and in purity. Until I come, devote yourself to the public reading of Scripture, to preaching and to teaching. Do not neglect your gift, which was given you through prophecy when the body of elders laid their hands on you. Be diligent in these matters; give yourself wholly to them, so that everyone may see your progress. Watch your life and doctrine closely. Persevere in them, because if you do, you will save both yourself and your hearers."[9]

I felt that this was a call of God to me. It was a message to Timothy, but I felt drawn by it. I believed that God had given me a gift just as he had to Timothy and that God was saying to me that I had to use it all the more. In my case the gift was teaching. I had used it at the Bible study and prayer meeting, but now I believed

---

[9] 1 Timothy 4:12-16

that God was instructing me to use it more widely. At the time, I interpreted this to be a call to the ministry. And that would require going to university.

I spoke to my minister about it, and he had misgivings, but told me to proceed in getting qualifications; the ones I had from school were now a few years old and no longer acceptable. I discovered that I had to go to technical college, so I handed in my notice to give up my job, got a grant from the Local Education Authority and went to Kirkcaldy College of Technology for a year. To keep travel costs down, I gave other students lifts and they shared the cost of the petrol with me. In this way I got to know them. I already knew one as he was the son of the deputy rector of the secondary school I had attended, and I knew him from the scouts. I had seen his father pick him up from there every Friday night. Every day, I drove to and from Kirkcaldy with a full car. I succeeded at getting the qualifications I needed and then I applied for university. I was accepted into the Arts Faculty of Glasgow University.

12

A New Beginning

It was the early 1980s. I attended Freshers' Week and I loved it. I made met Geoff, who was in the Science faculty and was the Christian Union Leader in the halls of residence. He was a few years younger than me, but I thought that he was very well taught. He was a member of the Brethren. We became good friends and he introduced me to other members of the Christian union.

Life was good. I had chosen my faculty and subjects, and I thought that after a few years I would enter the ministry, subject to being accepted as a candidate for the Church. I reasoned that if I had a degree and then dressed the part and presented myself in a manner that pleased those who did the selecting for the ministry, it would not be long before I would be in a pulpit.

When I had settled into my room, there was a knock at the door. There stood a bald man. He introduced himself as David, told me that he was the block warden and said that if I had any questions then I should come to him. He was in the room next to mine. Later I met with Geoff and some of the other students. I told them that David had introduced himself to me and they said that he was a Christian. I returned to my room and, once again, there was a knock at the door. There was David again.

"The other students have told me about you," I said.

"They have told me about you too!" he replied.

We then spoke of our faith in Jesus. I found that David was a man that I admired; a very good Bible teacher. He was a positive influence on all of us.

There were times when there would be a discothèque in the halls. When this happened, David would have an alternative evening in his room to which he would invite anyone in the Christian Union. I chose to attend those evenings. He would play recordings of various preachers. The recordings were on loan from a library. I wrote off to become a member of the library and get the recordings for myself. I did not realise at the time but by doing this, I was making contact with Operation Mobilisation. This was my second and, so far, most direct contact with them. God was using the library to draw me closer to himself and into a vastly different life to the one that I envisioned.

There were two student unions in the university. Originally, there had been one for the men and one for the women, but when I arrived, for the first time, both unions accepted men *and* women. I chose the one that was closer to most of my lectures, which had been the women's union. Sometimes things were promoted in the foyer that were not right in the eyes of God, but that was to be expected. I was in the world, but not a citizen of the world. My citizenship was in God's kingdom. The union was also a place of political activity. Many times I would enter the building to be greeted by young men selling the communist newspaper, the Morning Star, or once inside I would find pamphlets promoting the Liberal Party. I myself, though interested in politics, had no party allegiance. For me the union was purely functional. It was a place to sit down and have something to drink and do some study, and sometimes meet with friends. The hustle and bustle of activity made me wonder how some students ever found the time to study as they seemed to spend so much time fighting Party politics. It did, however, introduce me to how other people think. My life up until then had consisted almost entirely of the county of Fife and the occasional visit to Glasgow and Edinburgh, but here I was surrounded by very intelligent and interesting people from all over

Scotland, a few from England and some from other parts of the world. My little world was opening up. It was exciting.

I attended the main Scripture Union meetings. A fellow student addressed one of the meetings and concerning the overseas students he said, "I am just an ordinary Joe Bloggs but these people are the very best that their countries can produce, and they have sent them here to educate them. At the end of their time, they will graduate and return home. One day they will be the leaders of their countries, and while they are here, it is up to us to persuade them to trust in Christ so that when they go back they will be the missionaries in their own countries." I believed that he was right. We needed to seize every opportunity to communicate the gospel to the overseas students. One of them, when speaking to David, said that there was more opportunity to hear the gospel in Scotland than there was in his own country. This confirmed to me all the more the need to get alongside them.

Although I attended the main Christian Union meetings, I preferred the ones in the halls of residence. They were smaller, and we saw each other on a daily basis at meals or in each other's rooms. I also thought that we were privileged, as most students stayed at home and were not in a position to gather in smaller groups for Bible study and prayer as we were. For me, the hall of residence group was a learning curve. We all contributed to discussion at Bible study, which enhanced our fellowship. I quickly discovered that some students were very sincere and loved the Lord, but had not received the depth of teaching that I had in my church. I attempted to impart that to them. In that first year, I think we were a harmonious group. I always felt that David looked out for us not only as a group but as individuals. He cared for us and advised us well.

Many of the Christian students went to a particular church in the middle of Glasgow. David observed this and said that they were going to a good church where they would be taught well. However, as they were travelling to it, they passed by some smaller churches that were also very good, who would have gladly welcomed them. David said, "The closest Bible-believing church to your home is the one you should go to." Some churches have lost the gospel completely while others do not have the preaching of God's word as revealed in the Bible as a primary focus. Much prayer and wisdom is needed in making such a choice.

I discovered another church in the street where many of the students lived that opened every day to provide lunches for them. There was a door that led down to a basement room called The Crypt. I found this a convenient place for lunch as it was closer to the places I had my lectures in than either of the Union buildings. Also several members of the Christian Union went there, presumably for the same reason. Every day, I had scotch pie and baked beans, a princely feast indeed.

We would discuss serious spiritual issues. We did not agree on everything, but on the fundamentals we were united. We all knew that we were sinners. We all thought wrong things or did wrong things that were not pleasing to God, yet in his mercy, God the Father had sent his son Jesus to die in our place, and Jesus had risen from the dead. He was both God and man and he did not have sin. We rejoiced that God had shown such love to us.

Although The Crypt lunches were aimed at all students, most of those who came were members of the Christian Union. There was a programme called 'Table Talk' that Christian students could sign up to. This meant that at a given time they would have their lunch in one of the Student Unions and engage other students in conversation about Christ. For those who lived at home this was probably good training for them, but I did not participate in it. I did my 'table talking' to other students in the halls of residence every morning at breakfast and every night at dinner. We got to know some of them very well indeed and prayed that they too would trust in Jesus. One such student was Kathy.

Kathy, a music student, came from the North of Scotland, from a town I had never heard of. She had a lot of questions and we could tell that she had put a great deal of thought into the things she asked. We had a number of mutual friends. Anne, who was one of those mutual friends, came to me and said, "Guess who has become a Christian?" I knew immediately that she meant Kathy. I was so pleased. It seemed to me that from that day, Kathy went from someone who enquired about God to someone who grew and grew in spiritual stature. She needed a church, and Anne suggested that I ask Kathy if she would care to go with me. She accepted and she went to church with me every Sunday. Kathy had come to know God by thinking deeply about it and seizing ever opportunity to ask very well thought out questions that led to long discussions and encouraged the rest of us to get to know our bibles very well.

13

University Life

I loved university but I had a problem. In order to get my degree, I needed a language, and I had not studied any language at school or college. Therefore I was restricted to a dead language. My adviser told me to do Classical Greek. He himself was a language lecturer. I tried hard but I could not master it. I knew that if I put more effort into it then my other subjects would suffer. At the end of the year, I passed the other subjects but failed Greek. To meet the language requirement in my second year, my advisor told me to do Old English. It was a two-year course. I found that I was just as bad at this as I was at Greek. I started to feel demoralised. I hoped that at some point a solution would be found. In the meantime, I got on with my studies.

I found that I met people of all sorts, including those who were somewhat precocious. There was a lady some years older than me who was a student in my Moral Philosophy lectures. She told me that she knew someone who wanted my body. I laughed. I could not believe that anyone would approach me like that and be so brazen. She knew very little about me, but she knew she wanted sex and had decided to go for it. My laughter was enough of a refusal, but in that moment my whole life was in the balance – all I had been, my reputation, and all that might come. One can work for the Lord very hard yet a reputation can be destroyed in one foolish act.

There were other students who were God's instruments to work on me for good. Jools was one of them. He had been one of the first people I had met and he was another member of the Brethren. He related a conversation to me that he had had with another student, in which he had been told that there was no God and no need for God. Jools had told the other student that the difference between them was that he recognised his need. In my view that was a good way of putting it. I thought back to the day that I had been converted and had become aware that I was a sinful man. On the outside I seemed to be good, but inside I thought wrong things and God convicted me of this and brought me to the point where I realised that I was dead in sin and, contrary to appearances, depraved; and yet God had still chosen me. He had sent his son to die for me, Christ had risen from the dead, and I had trusted in him and been saved. Such was God's marvellous love to me, and to Jools, and to all who trust in him. Jools always referred to the Bible on any matter and not to his imagination. I have found this to be a good life discipline. Things that are not in the Bible may be open to opinion or to biblical principal, but where a matter is specifically in the Bible then we have to obey even if we do not like it or our emotions do not find what the Bible says appealing. I enjoyed spending time with him and talking about spiritual matters. He had a level of understanding of scripture that was not common, and I thought that he stood head and shoulders over many. He would often talk about passages in the Bible he had recently read and apply them to his life. He encouraged me at every opportunity.

Christopher came to the halls later than I did. He attended the Scripture Union meetings and was therefore familiar with the format. A book or letter from the Bible had been chosen for the whole term and passages from it were to be discussed. Someone would present the topic for discussion; there was no formal preaching. It fell to Christopher to present it one evening and in addition to the students who lived in the hall, he did two things that had never been done before. First he invited a large number of people from his church and second he gave a formal address.

What he had to say was by no means clear to me and, as it was intended to be a discussion, I interrupted by putting forward biblical points of view. One of the visitors challenged me on this and said that I should be quiet as Christopher was trying to present something. I said that it was meant to be a discussion. There was a deathly silence. The visitors had not realised that. I concluded that Christopher was well intentioned in what he had to say, but by inviting a large number of people from the church whom none of the rest of us knew, he was creating an opportunity to show to the church what a great speaker he believed himself to be. He was never asked to lead a meeting again. I, however, had made a mark. I was respected by at least some of my fellow students, but there was at least one individual among the visitors who warned Christopher to "watch out" for me. I was saddened by that as I would have done him no harm. I wanted him to learn that it is not a good idea to run before you can walk and he had been attempting to elevate himself rather than let events take their course and see where God would lead him in providence. It is always good to be humble before God, and I had to check my own heart as any one of us can be prone to being proud. If Christopher had asked if he could give a formal address and have some visitors, then that would have been a better approach than imposing it on us.

In the halls of residence, I made some close friends. I loved the fellowship of Geoff as I found that he was similar to me in terms of what he perceived as sound biblical teaching. It was he who had introduced me to Jools, whom I formed a similar opinion of, and Jools in turn introduced me to Jimmy. The four of us were very conservative in our thinking.

The year was coming to an end and a new Christian Union needed to elect a new leader as Geoff was not going to be living in the hall the following year. We prayed about it, and one man asked God to guide us in selecting the new leader – as God looks at the heart and not outward charisma. However, the new leader was to be selected by the executive CU committee, none of whom lived in the halls. In a private conversation Jools said to me, "It is about whom you know."

I had indeed observed that although we acted as though God chose the leaders, in fact people always supported their friends. For the most part that worked; however, such an approach has consequences. People can be selected because they are 'nice', but may not necessarily have suitable leadership qualities; and this is exactly what happened. God has given us the responsibility of choosing leaders and we should look for people who have the qualities necessary for it. God will not choose for us.

A charismatic church had opened near the university, and a number of students had been drawn to it. Some experienced the 'charismatic gifts' for the first time and were passionate about this to the extent that they wanted everybody else in the Christian Union to experience the same and agree with their theological viewpoint. For those of us of a conservative persuasion, this was never going to happen. We felt that whilst the group represented a broad spectrum of Christian belief, we were having a single perspective and opinion imposed on us.

Rather than deal with the issue directly, the leader of the hall Christian Union approached the central Christian Union leaders to find a solution, none of whom lived in the halls. I did not feel this would solve the problem and I was right; nothing happened. There was no attempt at guidance or discipline, which was what was needed. We lacked the clear, decisive leadership that was needed to ensure that the Christian Union would indeed be a *union*.

An emergency meeting of the Christian Union was called in the hall. I did not attend it, but another student – Alexander – emerged from it very angry. He told me that everybody had been instructed to "love one another". We discussed this together with David, the block warden, and all agreed that simply being told to love one another would make no difference. Love is practical, and therefore an admonishment to love needs to be accompanied by clear instructions as to how that love can be worked out in practice. Otherwise it can remain a purely romantic or sentimental concept – and in this case it had no effect.

David could not interfere in the running of the Christian Union, but he expressed to some of us privately that those of a more charismatic persuasion would be best to practise 'speaking in tongues' privately but not in the official Christian Union meetings. This wisdom was not communicated to everyone and for that I stand guilty. I should have presented that case, but as I was not the official leader, I did not take that stand. Even if it had been rejected, it would have been better to suggest it and see what people thought; perhaps then we would have learned more about loving one another.

There was another issue that I felt got in the way. It was planned that there would be a holiday on a barge, but the barge had restricted numbers so some people were not invited. It created a feeling of 'them and us'. I was not invited nor was anyone I felt close to. I thought that going on holiday was a good idea, but choosing one that we could not all go on was not wise.

We lived with the division for the whole year. I thought that it was awful, and it all stemmed from having a nice but weak, ineffective leader. The real trouble started with the belief that all leaders are chosen by God. But in the New Testament it is believers who appoint their own leaders; we live with the consequences of our choices, and then we commend them in prayer to God as the Apostles did.

14

Affairs of the Heart

Some of the students left the Halls of Residence to live elsewhere. I sat opposite two of the new female students at dinner on my first night back in the halls of residence at the start of a new academic year. One of them was a girl with lovely long red hair. I thought she was gorgeous. She had a gentle personality and I felt something tug at my heart. Mary was a Christian and quickly got to know the Christian Union. She was a minister's daughter from a small town in the North of Scotland. Once again, I found it exciting to meet someone from another part of the country that I had never been to. I thought Mary was one of the most beautiful and delightful people I had ever seen. I wanted to be with her. There were, however, two problems. Firstly, someone else had already asked her out. Secondly, being the daughter of a minister in the Church of Scotland, Mary had paid the price of that. A congregation makes demands on a pastor's time, sometimes at the cost of his family, and Mary felt that. I wanted to be a Church of Scotland minister and therefore, although I personally seemed attractive to her, she did not want to be involved with me in that way. I, however, would not see reason and still pursued her; I would not take no for an answer. I thought, "If only I pray hard enough, she will see reason and God will give her to me." I just would not face the fact that although my heart belonged to her, and I told her so, she was never going to agree. During one holiday we wrote letters to each other and she sought counselling from her father. I have to say that he was very gracious, and when she wrote to me, during the summer holidays, she gently explained that the problem was in me. She was right, but I did not accept that at the time.

That year was a disaster. There was a painful division in the Christian Union and I was struggling academically because of my failure to come to grips with languages. My feelings for Mary were also a major distraction to study. I thought that if only I could cement a good relationship with her, then study would follow and, sooner or later, I would also get to grips with languages. None of these things happened. Instead, I was suspended from study for a year during which I had a reprieve. I had to re-do everything from the previous year and sit the exams again – this time at home and without a grant.

I had to register as unemployed – a humiliating experience. I saw myself as a reasonably intelligent and talented young man, but signing that register made me realise that society took a very different view of me. Interviews were stressful, and I still had the goal of becoming a Church of Scotland minister. Every time I went in to sign on to receive benefit, I feared that my finance would suddenly be cut off and my life would end. The stress was very great indeed. To make it worse, my brother Jim got a job in the Benefits Office. I dreaded that a day would come when my file would be on a desk in front of him. God in his providence spared me that, but I did see Jim at the next desk many times when I walked in there. We did not acknowledge each other. It was our way of coping with the situation.

I felt awful. I still could not get Mary out of my head and being at home, I felt trapped. I tried to get attached to someone else instead, but once again it was not to be.

One evening there was a knock at the door. There stood Judy – someone I had known from the Ranch Bible studies. I had met her through a mutual friend and had taken both of them to Ranch. Judy lived with her mother, and they had moved from the village they had lived in to the town and had started attending my church. She told me that the pastor had sent her to see me. I invited her in and she sat down. She seemed nervous. I can only describe what she had to say as sounding like a babble. It did not make any sense to me; all I understood was that she was talking about a man. When she left, I still had no understanding of what the issue was. As the pastor had sent her to see me, I phoned him. He asked me if I would like to come to his house the following day.

As I sat in the front room, I wondered what the pastor would say. I had sat in that same room for parties and to discuss my own problems. This was different. He sat down and told me what Judy had discussed with him before he had sent her to see me. As I listened to him, it all made sense. The man she had referred to was me. She had romantic feelings for me. I had had no idea about that up to this point. It was a shock. I also realised that I could never return those feelings. She was a good friend but nothing more, and not the sort of person who had the sort of intellectual capacity that I would need in a life partner. I therefore told the minister that I would not be able to enter into such a relationship with her. I did, however, have to do something about it. She would have to be told.

The pastor suggested that he would invite both of us to his house; I would tell her that I could not have a romantic relationship with her and then I would leave, after which he would talk to her. I realised this would damage the friendship I had with her, but it had to be done. I was right; it did damage the friendship. She could not talk to me after that. I understood why because of my own experience. My feelings for Mary had been just the same, and likewise with another woman. However, this time it had been the other way round. I felt so bad about it but it was the only thing I could do. It made me review my behaviour in relationships and face some grim reality, which was that there is no point in pursuing someone who does not feel the same way. It only does harm. Although Judy and her mother continued to attend the church, the friendship was not what it had once been. It became and remained much more distant. However, I felt that I had learned from this incident and it had been good for me. It took courage to tell the truth that there was no hope of having the relationship with her that she wanted.

I made a feeble attempt at passing exams to return to university, but in my heart I knew that it was not going to happen. Signing on at an unemployment office is always depressing. I felt like I was going downhill every time I went in there. This black period of my life was to last several years. I felt my youth was being wasted.

There were times when the unemployment office would call me in for an interview to discuss job searches. For the most part, this was a formality. As long as I produced evidence of looking for work, they would go through the motions. That is what it felt like – just going through motions, but with no reality to it.

There were times when these interviews were just terrible. One of them was particularly bad. I sat in front of the desk. Behind it was a man in his twenties. I thought he was the sort who just hated his job and hated all the interviewees, especially the one who was sitting in front of him now. He made no eye contact, which made me uncomfortable. In fact it was clear that he was deliberately avoiding making eye contact with me. He was emotionally detached and his choice of words was appalling. For example, he said that if I did not do something soon they would get the thumbscrews out. I already felt bad enough without such a remark.

I could not accept my university failure and was determined that, no matter how hard it was, I was going to make a success of it. I applied to the Open University and also acquired funding for it. This was in God's providence for me. It is remarkable that the Fife region financially supported me. Studying gave me a sense of purpose and hope: I would get a degree, but this time I would study subjects that I was good at and enjoyed so that I would succeed.

I saw an advert for a Wycliffe Bible Translators' conference to be held at Crieff, a town about thirty-three miles from where I lived. I could just about scrape enough money together to go. The conference lasted for a weekend. I met the organiser, and we became friends. That conference opened my eyes to the worldwide mission field. I met people at it who had gone out from Scotland to other parts of the world, and listening to them talking about the work they were doing and praying for them expanded my vision for God's purposes. Up until then, I had only prayed for things and people around Scotland; I realised that I had been very inward-looking. This was much bigger, and exciting. I knew I could not be a Wycliffe Bible Translator because of my negative experience of language learning at University. However, I did think that if I ever became a minister in the Church of Scotland, I would want to keep a link with the Wycliffe Bible Translators and encourage them. I would promote them in any church where I was minister. I went to several of these conferences over the years and felt like I was part of an extended worldwide family.

I became more interested in other missions and started to receive their prayer letters. One such letter was very significant to me and resulted in a rather unusual experience. I received a small stack of letters that had been delivered that morning. I laid them aside with the intention of reading them later. However, I had a feeling that stirred inside me as soon as I put them down. I felt an urgent need to open them *now*, because I sensed that in one of them there was something about Dunfermline. I picked up the letters, tore them open and scanned quickly through them looking for Dunfermline and, to my astonishment, I found it. 'Youth With A Mission' (YWAM) were going to have a 'Summer of Service' with a church at the bottom of the town. I knew the pastor and his wife for they had pastored the Pentecostal Church just over the hill from our house and I had met them through a school friend. In the days when I was singing in the band, we had played a few times at the Pentecostal Church. On reading the letter, I found that YWAM were looking for volunteers to participate in the outreach. I had never done anything like that before and I wanted to participate. I replied to the letter and was accepted.

At the start of the mission, I went to the church and was greeted by the pastor and his wife and then met the other members of the team and, in particular, the YWAM couple who would be leading us. Those who were members of YWAM all came from the

USA, except one young lady who was from Canada. I loved being on a team that had people who had come from outside of Scotland. The main activities of the outreach were praying for the district and going door to door to talk to people. This can be a very uncomfortable experience. We also campaigned to get children to come to the church during the day, where we would teach them Bible lessons.

I was very moved when a little girl who was sitting on my lap managed to get her hand inside the sleeve of my shirt and she stroked my arm. I asked her if she wanted me to put her down. She shook her head, as she continued to stroke my arm. Later, I told one of the girls on the team about this. She said, "She probably wanted to stroke your arm because she does not have a father and does not know what a man feels like." That had not occurred to me. Sometimes a simple act reveals a great deal.

When you are on a team, you have a common goal. Anyone who is not focussed on the goal is a distraction. I thought that one of the young men on the team was flirtatious and had an eye for the ladies, with little or no interest in the mission. I said nothing about this, but the team leader must have also spotted it as he told us that he had asked the man to leave and was not going to give us any reasons. I believed he was right to do this as team discipline is important. People on a team need to be there for all the right reasons, and it seemed to me that this young man was not. From that point on, the team were more focussed on the goal of reaching out to the community without relationships getting in the way.

As I had now established face-to-face contact with YWAM, I decided to go on one of their Discipleship Training Weeks. This was a taster for their Discipleship Training School. I enjoyed the week and met some interesting people. One was a butcher who had been a 'bit of a bad lad' and God had turned him around. Another was an older man from a nearby town, and still another was a young man who had turned from his immorality.

One of the subjects that we addressed that week was 'Rejection'. This proved to be a major focus for one man, because he loved the Lord with all his heart and his girlfriend had rejected him saying that he was too spiritual for her. He mentioned her in prayer a lot during the week. Evidently he still felt raw from her rejection. In one instance, I was walking behind him going to the dining room when he turned round and asked me if I had been rejected. I think that in asking that question he saw in me a kindred spirit. I said yes, as I did feel rejected by people I had loved and that had led at least in part to my unemployment – or at least that is what I thought at the time.

It was during the Discipleship Training Week that we received some bad news. Operation Mobilisation had two ships, the Logos and the Doulos. We were told that the Logos had run aground off the coast of Chile and the crew had abandoned ship. I wondered how God could allow such a thing to happen. These were people just like us seeking to serve him, and this disaster had befallen them. We prayed for the safety of the crew. God answered that prayer; every one of them got off the ship safely. I did not know at the time that some of the people on that ship would one day be my friends.

My experience of Youth With A Mission and Wycliffe Bible Translators deepened my interest in Christian mission. They set me up for what was to follow.

15

Mission Experience

It was decided that my church should have summer missions. To that end we approached the Scripture Union to run them. They supplied us with a leader, and some young people from the church became the outreach team. I was among them. I had found the YWAM outreach a positive experience and now I had the opportunity to do a similar thing for my own church. I participated in several of these, but the first one was most memorable as we had a number of young people who came over from Northern Ireland to help us. Once again I found that I enjoyed working alongside people from outside of Scotland.

Those of us who were members of the church were on the planning team. The Scripture Union leader would also attend those meetings in the lead up to the outreach. In this way it was the church who planned the mission, not the Scripture Union. We did a mailshot round the district making parents aware that there would be a holiday club that their children could attend.

We were very successful at getting large numbers of children. It was like running an enormous Sunday school, for many of the lessons taught were just like Sunday school lessons. Scripture Union supplied us with scripts for a series of sketches on biblical themes, which the team performed. My most memorable one was that each day I would appear dressed as Percy the Parrot. For this I had to wear tights. The team leader told me to wear different coloured tights every day so that when he ran the quiz, one of the questions would be, "What colour were Percy's legs today?" It was fun and it taught me about communicating.

I added to my mission experience by attempting to join London City Mission. I spent a week at their voluntary evangelistic base getting a taste for it. A programme for the week had been worked out for me. Each day I went to a different mission station. Some of them looked after the down-and-outs by feeding them. I had never done this sort of work before and it was an eye-opener. The gospel would be preached to them and often this would take the form of a discussion. Some of them were intelligent people who argued with the London City Missionary who was leading the meeting. As one of the missionaries put it to me, "They have a lot of skill; you have to admire the ability they have to be able to survive on the streets."

As we served up a simple lunch, I felt the need to go to the toilet. I asked one of the regular volunteers where it was.

"We keep one for ourselves on the top floor," she replied.

"Yes," I said, "but where is the nearest?"

She repeated her answer and once again I asked where the nearest one was.

"Some of them suffer from syphilis," she explained, "so we keep one for ourselves on the top floor."

This brought the discussion to an end and I promptly went to the top floor!

I was not accepted for London City Mission so my unemployment continued. Going to the unemployment office every two weeks to sign on continued to be a drudge, made even worse when I expected I would see my brother among the staff. Being called in for an interview was by far the worst part of the experience. I started to appreciate simple things that were an excuse to get out of the house for a while.

Three of the churches had cafes that I visited, each one different in character. I knew people in all of them. It was a blessed relief to spend a little time with them and to forget about my situation for a short time. The people were kind but none of them had experience of what I was going through. I was just grateful that they were there. They gave me a spiritual and emotional lift that I needed just by their presence. In one of them I discovered a man who was the father of a boy and girl whom I had been at school with. I had met his children in my final year in the school Scripture Union, so I could talk to him about them. He made it his business to sit at the tables and talk to people. He told me that people would come in and want to unburden themselves and just talk about their cares, and he would listen. I was clearly one of those people. I loved getting to know him. I had loved his children and now I loved him. I could see that as a Christian man he had been a very good example to them. They were just as loving and caring as him. I also got to know other people in these cafes whom I grew to love. They knew they were not just serving tea and coffee. They were doing a work for God's kingdom, and there were many who needed it. For some, they knew nothing of God and it was an opportunity to get to know them. For me, it was just lovely to get out of the house and spend time with people. Without them, I think my morale would have sunk like a stone.

16

The Red Light District

There are times when I read prolifically. In the early 1990s I bought a book by a well-known member of Youth With A Mission, chiefly because a large part of the book is about his life in the red light district of Amsterdam. When I finished it, I received a letter from a friend whom I had met when I was attempting to become a London City Missionary. He had been one of the volunteer evangelists. The letter said that he was working in a Christian Youth Hostel in the red light district of Amsterdam and invited me to come out there to work beside him. The fact that I had just read about it, and now I had this letter of invitation, was one of those God-ordained decision times. Apart from a flight in a light aircraft when I was a child with my brother and father round Blackpool tower, I had never flown before. I had also never considered going to the red light district. All my mission experience was in the UK, and the red light district was daunting. I had read about the drug pushers, pimps and prostitutes; I realised life there would be grim. My first instinct was to say, "No, I cannot cope." However, I delayed replying for a few days to think about it.

The book contained a lot of frightening experiences. I did not think that I was of the same calibre as the author and his family who had endured so much to minister there. I was terrified.

However, I reasoned with myself that reading a book is one thing, but no book, no matter how good, can give anyone experience. I therefore decided to make a compromise. I had been a member of the Youth Hostels Association for some years and was therefore familiar with hosteling. I wrote to my friend and told him that I would come to the hostel for a week as a guest to see what it was like. My plan was that I would find out for myself if I could cope or not and then I would make a final decision. Eventually I decided on a date that meant that I would be in the hostel over Christmas.

I found the district a deep and very dark shade of red both physically and spiritually. It seemed like the devil was in control of the place. It was just as the book described. There were windows with red lights above them and young women wearing very little, to entice men to come in, gambling with their health and lives. As one man put it to me, the clients risk everything for half an hour of pleasure. Drugs were rife, especially in the public houses that were called coffee shops.

There were, however, places of refuge from all this. One was The Cleft. I had read about it and decided to seek it out. It was a place run by YWAM in the middle of the district. I found it, and it seemed to me as an oasis would be to a thirsty man, a good break from all the temptations around me. I felt that all of my senses were being assaulted at one and the same time. One could ignore the girls in the windows but I soon discovered that there were others, nick-named 'Coke Queens' because of their addiction to drugs, who walked the streets and would directly approach men. Looking at all this made me feel that the devil was laughing as he caused so much pain destroying people lives.

My main fear was that I would have drug-pushers in the streets trying to force me to buy drugs all the time. This never happened. All I had to do was walk on. The district not only had a distinct look, it also had its smells. The Dutch are very fond of cheese and there are small shops that sell many varieties of it. The smell was pleasant and it wafted out into the streets. There was also another smell; it was lovely, but I soon learned it was a bad sign. As a non-smoker, I have always found the smell of tobacco disgusting, but here I could pass by men who were smoking and I found it pleasant. It was not tobacco but hash. The hostel had a strict rule about this. No guest was permitted to come into the hostel under the influence of drugs and there should be no dealing. If drugs were found on the premises, they were to be handed over to the management and the guest expelled.

Christmas away from home in the red light district was very different to the ones I was accustomed to. The hostel closed to normal business on Christmas Day, and all the staff and guests had Christmas dinner in the dining room. The general manager was chairman of the festivities. I found a seat at a table next to my friend who had invited me. At every place was a small package wrapped in Christmas paper. I was curious to know what was inside, so I unwrapped the one at my place. It contained a small white object. "A strange-looking chocolate," I thought, and I attempted to bite a piece. Then I spat it out! I thought that I had never tasted anything so disgusting in my life. It was revolting!

Christmas dinner consisted of turkey with all the trimmings. It was delicious! During the meal, the general manager stood up to speak. All eyes were upon him and all ears listening intently to what he was about to say. He welcomed all of us to the Christmas meal; then he talked about Christmas and how lovely it is. There are the carols, the gifts, and at Christmas we remember how God sent his son. Thinking about Jesus as a helpless baby is a lovely thought. He likened it to the small packages we had found at our dinner places. The Christmas paper made them look pretty, just like Christmas itself. He then said that if we would take the paper off, we would find something ugly inside. He said that he had just seen someone attempt to eat one of them. (I had thought myself very discreet when attempting to eat it!) He said that they were tulip bulbs. I am not a gardener, so I had not recognised it for what it was.

He likened the ugly tulip bulb to being the other side of Christmas, the thing we do not like to think about or talk about: *Easter.* At Easter we are reminded that the gentle baby in the cradle became a man, who was brutally put to death on our behalf. We like to think of a cute little baby, but we do not like to think of the blood from the stripes on his back where he was scourged, or the holes in his hands and feet where the nails were hammered though his body to hang him on the cross, or the blood from the wounds on his head where they placed a crown of thorns. Yet this was done for us. His body was then put in a tomb and he rose from the dead on the third day, as the Bible says.[10] The general manager picked up the tulip bulb by his plate and then went on to say that if we take this ugly thing and bury it in soil, as we do with the dead, it grows into a beautiful flower. Similarly, Jesus died, was buried and rose again. If we trust in him to save us from our sin, we will not face the wrath of God. We will have eternal life with him – and now is the time to accept his gift of eternal life.

I not only found his address to be truthful, I found it deeply moving and memorable. I thought it was one of the best presentations of the gospel that I had ever heard.

I enjoyed my week at the hostel. I had seen the district and experienced something of it. I now had to make a decision. Would I go and work in the hostel or not? My week had confirmed that some of the things I was afraid of would not be a problem for me. I therefore decided to apply to spend three months there prior to applying for the Church of Scotland. This decision was to affect the rest of my life.

---

[10] e.g. 1 Corinthians 15:4

17

Back to the Red Lights

I packed my bags and flew to Amsterdam. I took a train from the airport to the city centre and as I was walking to the Shelter, I saw two police officers at a tram stop arresting a man. I had never seen someone being arrested before. "This is life in the city," I thought.

I continued on my way until I reached the hostel. There I entered the great double doors and was greeted by the receptionist, to whom I introduced myself. She told me to put my bags in the passageway behind her. As I did this, I noticed a man approaching who was behaving in a manner that indicated to me that he was going to proposition her. This was the red light district after all and in the eyes of many, any woman would be fair game. I stayed round the corner out of sight, just in case the receptionist needed my help. I heard her say, "We are a Christian Youth Hostel. We do not do that here." Evidently I was right; he was indeed propositioning her, but her reply was firm and final and she did not need my help.

I had arrived on a weekend and I had a couple of days to settle in. I assumed that I could spend those two days meeting the staff and then on the Monday I would start and they could see what an asset I was going to be to the hostel. In every avenue of life, be it Scripture Union, Youth Fellowship or university, I had been loved and respected. I thought that the Shelter would be just the same and that all the difficulties that I expected to encounter would come from the people in the streets or guests. However, I came to appreciate the truth of the Bible verse that says, "Be alert and of sober mind. Your enemy the devil prowls around like a roaring lion looking for someone to devour."[11] For indeed I quickly discovered that the devil sought to devour me and bring me down very quickly indeed, but his weapon for doing so was one that I was totally unprepared for. The weapon he used was not the pimps, the prostitutes or the drug dealers, but people on the Shelter staff, the very people I was introducing myself to, smiling at and expecting to get along well with.

The general manager, Fieke, came to me and asked me to come to the office. He wanted to speak to me. I recognised him from the Christmas dinner. As I sat down, he began by saying, "I have a problem with you..." This was a shock to me! I had no idea why he had said that or what was to follow. The conversation that followed seemed to take a long time. He said that four of the girls had come to him and complained about me. They had said that I was "weird". He did not go into details, except to say that he had asked them if I had made a pass at them. They had confirmed that I had not attempted to do so, but they still felt that I was weird. Inside, my soul just sank. I had done nothing wrong, nothing that I thought could offend anyone. On the contrary, I was attempting to make friends. However, he said that he would let me start and would talk to me in a couple of days. This made things very difficult indeed. I had no idea who had made the accusations against me and I was expected to work with these people. I started work in the snack bar cleaning and frying French fries and burgers.

After a couple of days Fieke came to me again and was still not satisfied. I had prayed with all my heart that the situation would be rectified and that I would hear nothing about it again, but here it was. I knew that I was on the verge of being sent home in disgrace and I still did not know why.

---

[11] 1 Peter 5:8

I cried a great deal. I decided that I needed to talk to someone, and I had met another manager called Dave, who was from the USA. I had only spoken to him once but I thought anyone would do, for I needed to pour my heart out to someone or I would break. We sat down in the office and I told him about the conversation that had taken place between Fieke and me. Dave listened very carefully to what I had to say, in between the sobs of tears as I spoke. I explained that I had come to the Shelter in all sincerity to serve the Lord and that I had no idea why such dreadful things were being said about me.

Then Dave said something I did not expect to hear, but it gave me a little hope: "When I came here, I was accused of being the loud-mouthed American." Dave had not always been one of the managers; he had been one of the cleaners. I thought, "This man started from the bottom and he understands my situation." He said that he would go and speak to Fieke, and I should wait while he went to see him. I sat there alone, wondering what the conversation between Dave and Fieke would be like and praying that it would go well so that I could stay and prove my worth.

Dave returned and said that there would be another meeting later that day. This time it would be in the courtyard and it would be Dave, Fieke and myself.

The time for the meeting came, and we sat there with all the guests around us in the courtyard talking. I could not hold back the tears. I really wanted to go to somewhere more private to discuss things but there was nowhere in the building that was available. Dave asked Fieke if the girls had said anything specific. He said they had. They had said I was "weird", "talked too much" and was "not up to the job". I felt even more hurt by that last remark as I had not started the job when the allegations were made and therefore I considered the remark to be completely unfounded. Moreover, I had already done a great deal of work in the Lord's name with several churches. I felt that it was a lie.

After a while Fieke said that he and Dave were going to go inside and discuss it, and when he came back he would give me his final decision. That statement was clear: one way or another the situation was going to draw to a close. Either I was going to stay or go home in disgrace feeling betrayed. I sat alone among the crowd in the courtyard in the sunshine that normally I would have enjoyed, but I felt so bad that I was pouring out my heart to the Lord in prayer.

At last Fieke emerged and sat beside me. Gently he said, "I have listened to what Dave has to say, and I have reached the conclusion that he is right. He even said that you have more good reasons to be here then he has." I felt like a great burden had fallen off my shoulders. The Lord had answered my prayers. All the stress was gone. I was so relieved. He then went on to say, "I am going to close the Shelter this afternoon. I will call a staff meeting in the snack bar. You will tell your life story, and they will be told that you are staying and that will be the end of the matter." For the first time since I arrived, I was looking forward to a staff meeting. Before coming to the hostel, I could not have imagined how important my first staff meeting would be, nor that I would be the focus of attention at it.

Fieke was as good as his word. The Shelter closed and all the staff met in the snack bar. He said that some allegations had been made against me and now I was going to address the staff. I told them of my spiritual journey up to that point. I also addressed the issue of the allegation that I talked too much. I said that whilst I perhaps do talk a lot, I also remain silent when I am listening to people as they have things that they may wish to say to me. I said that if they would give me a chance, they would discover that.

In closing, Fieke explained that some people are a little different and we need to get along with them. Then the meeting came to an end. I was indeed staying. The devil had fought and lost. I still believe that it was because of prayer that I was enabled to stay. I had learned about prayer in the prayer meetings of my church. Now I had experienced God's love through prayer at a far deeper level than I ever had before.

When I chose to talk to Dave, I had no idea that he had suffered allegations against himself too. In God's providence, I had spoken to the only other person who was going to be able to help me. I was overjoyed. I thanked the Lord many times and to this day I still do. In desperation I had cried out to the Lord and he had listened to me. The Bible says that God will honour those who honour him.[12] God accepted my prayers in difficult circumstances, and I learned from this that he can be depended on. What he says he will do. We must be humble and seek him for his guidance and accept whatever answer he gives. In my case, he opened the door for me to continue.

[12] 1 Samuel 2:30

18

Getting On With the Task

A special management meeting took place. It was made clear that some changes would come into effect. Afterwards a notice was posted on the staff noticeboard that began with the words, "Are you curious?" It then announced the date and time of the next staff meeting at which the changes would be announced. Two things came out of it. Fieke was going on holiday and Gerla was joining the management. Gerla was the receptionist who had been on duty when had I first arrived and whom I heard being propositioned by a man. She would be taking up her new duties immediately and Fieke prayed for her that she might be able to sleep at night after work and not worry about any decisions she made. Although the issue about the accusations against me had been resolved, emotionally I still felt raw. I had not asked which girls had accused me as I did not want to know. I did not want to bear a grudge against anyone.

Fieke went on holiday and there were many times when Gerla was in charge and would sit at the head of the table at the staff evening meal. At one of those meals, she smiled at me and called me Georgio. I knew from the smile she was joking. What for her was a joke meant a great deal to me. It marked the start of a friendship that I needed. This kind woman extended her friendship to me and trusted me. As the weeks went by I grew to love her company. Some of the other girls had been shocked by the accusations against me and knew nothing about it. They trusted me, and I in turn loved and trusted them, but God's principal instrument in building that trust in me was Gerla. God knew how much I needed her.

When Fieke returned from holiday, I assumed that he would get a report about me. Evidently I was right, for he came to me and said very gently, "You have done well." If he had ever doubted letting me stay, his fears had been allayed. I also felt close to him. He was described by one girl as a "wise old owl". She was right. In the weeks to come, I found him to be a man of great godly wisdom.

In the mornings I would get up, go down to the snack bar and lay out cereals, milk and yogurt. I found that the Dutch love large quantities of plain yoghurt into which they add fruit. The main cereal was muesli. Breakfast was then topped off with bread and cheese. The bread was kept in freezers that were down in a cellar. Vast quantities of bread had to be served every day, so at the close of each day we would get bread out of the freezers to allow it to defrost overnight. One by one the guests would come in and help themselves and wash it down with coffee. I found that the Dutch love strong coffee.

A main meal would be cooked at night, usually consisting of meat and a couple of vegetables. When it was finished, I would go down to the cellar to get burgers and French fries out of the freezer, then fire up the deep fryer to cook the French fries and grill the burgers. These were done to order and would be served for the rest of the evening. Sometimes I cooked loompia, which is otherwise called Chinese Egg Roll. This was very popular with guests. It came frozen so all I had to do was heat it up in a microwave oven. I also cooked omelettes as they were ordered. These too were very popular.

I found that serving food was good for getting to meet all the guests. When I was not doing that, but circulating among them to talk to them, they all recognised me as the young man who had served them their meals. Most of them were willing to sit down, relax and talk. It was as though serving meals opened doors into their lives. They had seen me in action and had built up some trust in me. I was there like the rest of the staff to present Jesus Christ to them in a district that drew many people down into the depths of hurt and despair.

The toilets had blue lights. It is difficult to see veins under a blue light, so this was to prevent guests shooting themselves up with drugs. Every night a man would be left on duty to do the laundry, look after reception and, if there were any issues during the night, he was available to deal with them. One of them was Ebbs, a man from Africa. He often got this job and in the morning he would come to the staff lounge to make some breakfast for himself and tell us what had happened during the night. It seemed to me that things always happened when he was on duty and he faithfully dealt with them.

One morning he told us that he had seen a guest go into the toilet during the night and remain there for a long time. Finally Ebbs had gone in and found the man in a cubical. Ebbs looked down under the door, which had a gap between the bottom of the door and the floor.

"Excuse me," said Ebbs, "what are you doing?"

"Nothing," replied the man.

"Excuse me," said Ebbs, "you have something in your hand."

"No I do not," said the man.

"Excuse me, I insist that you *do* have something in your hand. Please drop it!"

The man dropped something.

"Excuse me," Ebbs said again, "you *still* have something in your hand."

This time the man dropped everything. Ebbs was right. He was attempting to take drugs and he had to leave the hostel.

This was by no means an isolated incident. I sometimes found packets of drugs on tables. We had to set a standard of behaviour in the hostel that was not found outside in the streets. We had to be seen to stand apart from the world around us. Ebbs enforced the rules politely but firmly. He was also very popular with the staff. We respected him.

19

Life in the District

Somehow I had to cope with the district. I knew about the Youth With A Mission meetings in The Cleft and I discovered that they had a barge where they also held meetings. I thought that it would be good to go to these places where I could meet fellow believers who were not working at the Shelter; but to get there I had to walk through the narrow streets. Some of the streets were so narrow that they were really just alleyways. I quickly discovered that as I passed by, the sight of any man was enough to make the girls in the windows knock on them to get my attention. I found that the best thing to do was to keep walking briskly. The Bible passage about committing adultery in your heart if you so much as gaze upon a woman[13] seemed to burn in my head.

I went to The Cleft many times. Sometimes the walk there was easier than at other times. If I knew that a woman on the staff at the Shelter was also going there, I would walk with her. In this way I was focussed on where I was going, and the presence of a woman stopped the girls knocking on the windows. I went with one of the cleaners on one occasion – a tall, beautiful blonde girl from Sweden. As we walked she looked around at the windows and then looked

---

[13] Matthew 5:28

at me and smiled. She said, "I am protecting you now." I knew it was true.

Each time I went to The Cleft, there was a certain prostitute who would be walking in the street outside. Every time I saw her, she seemed to be getting more and more ill. Her skin turned grey. She had red, horizontal marks on the backs of her legs across the calves. I realised that the only thing that could make marks like that was a car bumper; someone had run her down with a car. One of the cleaners at the Shelter told me that incidents like that are not unknown; some people hate the prostitutes.

One day she was not outside. I entered The Cleft and there she was sitting at a table at the back of the room, head down and crying. She was in utter despair. More people arrived for the meeting. As the meeting went on, the girl left. The man leading the meeting made an announcement. He said, "I feel that I should say something about the young lady who was at the back." He went on to say, "She is very ill and my wife has taken her to the hospital." She needed help and she got it from God's people. She had plied her trade just outside a place where God's people met and where she in turn could meet with God.

Every night when not on duty, the Shelter staff would have dinner together round a large table in the staff room. The duty manager that evening would sit at the head of the table and lead a short devotional before the meal. It was often a reading from the Bible, along with a few thoughts concerning the passage that had just been read. It was to one of those meals that a particular woman was invited. I recognised her immediately. She was a prostitute who walked the streets at the back of the Samaritans Inn, a Christian café I sometimes went to on the outskirts of the district. Dave and another man introduced her and said that she was a friend of theirs. We had a lovely meal, and what I enjoyed most of all about it was the respect that was shown to that girl. We, as a community of God's people, had to act differently from the world.

The next day, I went to the Samaritans Inn, and there she was at the back of it.

"Hello, would you like to have sex with me?" she invited.

"You do not recognise me, do you?" I replied.

She shook her head.

"You had dinner with us last night," I said.

She was silent. Then we talked for a short time.

A few weeks later, she was booked into the Shelter as a guest with the backing of a certain government agency. From that day on I never saw her at the back of the Samaritans Inn again or in any other part of the district. She was a guest at the Shelter for a number of weeks. At the time, I was of the opinion that she was doing what she could to get out of prostitution and that being introduced to us that evening at dinner had been the start of it. Once again, God's people were doing what they could for someone who needed it.

I had read about the Samaritans Inn before coming to Amsterdam. I went there to get away from the daily pressure of the Shelter.

One day I was drinking coffee, feeling not a little afraid, when this verse came to my mind: "One night the Lord spoke to Paul in a vision: 'Do not be afraid; keep on speaking, do not be silent. For I am with you, and no one is going to attack and harm you, because I have many people in this city.'"[14] The Apostle Paul had been just as afraid as I was and the Lord gave him reassurance. I knew there were many fellow believers around me. I was sitting among some of them and I gained confidence in the work.

Sometimes the Inn would be closed so that Bible studies could take place without being interrupted by customers. It came as something of a shock to me to find that at one study there was a man who looked like he could rip my head off. He wore leathers from head to foot with all sorts of decorations on them including studs, and the sides of his head were shaven. In the middle of it was an enormous tomahawk hairstyle that consisted of what seemed like all the colours of the rainbow. We put tables together in the middle of the inn for all of us to sit round and this man led the Bible study. The way he looked was not my idea of what a believer in Christ normally looked like, and yet the manner in which he spoke was so

---

[14] Act 18:9-10

gentle, and he gave sound biblical warnings about sin. I had no doubt in my mind that this man loved the Lord. His appearance was of no consequence. I expect that many found him as surprising as I did, and there are subcultures that probably accepted him more readily as he would be one of their own. For me, it was a fascinating experience to meet such a person. He talked about being filled with the Holy Spirit. He said of the red light district, "If you are looking in the windows, you are not walking in the Holy Spirit." To be filled means to be self-controlled. These studies were good for me.

There was an older man, who faithfully served regularly behind the bar. William did not speak English well, but he spoke enough for me to understand him and for him to understand what customers were ordering. Like all the staff at the Inn, he was a believer, but not one of those who sat at the tables engaging customers in conversation. As many customers were tourists, they spoke in English, but William could not enter into conversations about Jesus because of his poor grasp of the language. However, I saw in him a man who was faithful. He deeply loved God and was doing what he could to reach others by working behind the bar. It was possible to chat to him at the bar, and pouring coffee was the skill God had given him to serve in his kingdom. He seemed to be of retirement age, yet here he was in a place full of young people. He was clearly very fond of many of them and they in turn loved him. He would see to it that customers got a leaflet that would explain the way of salvation. Many of the customers came from other parts of the country and the world. He was determined to reach as many people as he could with the gospel by any means that was at his disposal, and he did not show favour to anyone or despise anyone who came in. He just showed the love of Jesus to everyone who came through the door. Some of the time we learn life's lessons just by watching others and aspiring to be like them in as much as they are like Jesus.

20

Valuable Lessons

Christians are sinners. We are saved, but we are still battling that inner old man who is selfish. It comes out in a variety of ways. Lunchtimes at the Shelter could be one of those ways. Bread, cheese, butter and a variety of other foods for sandwiches would be laid out on the table for people to eat. We would take what we wanted, sit down and talk. The conversations tended to be about the guests or the staff. At a staff meeting Fieke mentioned how much we were eating for lunch and that it was costing too much. None of us had ever taken that into consideration. When one does not have to think about paying, the selfish inner old man, the sinful nature, will take and take and take, and that was what was going on. To resolve this issue, Fieke instructed us regarding the quantities that each one of us could take. In this way, we all got lunch, everything was distributed fairly and the food budget was brought under control.

I found that practical issues like this are in fact spiritual ones. God had entrusted the resources to us. It was also good discipline, learning to respect our leaders on seemingly small practical matters as well as bigger ones. Sometimes our perspective is an illusion. All matters are big if our actions are detrimental to others.

By only taking the prescribed amounts of food, we were showing love to one another. I was reminded of how the Bible says, "Catch for us the foxes, the little foxes that ruin the vineyards, our vineyards that are in bloom."[15] By telling us exactly what quantities we could eat, Feike was dealing with the spiritual little foxes that would destroy the fellowship among us.

Staff meetings were a steep learning curve for me. I had my first experience of culture shock. The British tend to be diplomatic when dealing with disagreements. The Dutch tackle it head on and confront it, and if one is not accustomed to that, it can be emotionally draining.

The Shelter had a number of beds set aside for homeless young people. They would come and spend a few weeks in safety where they knew they would be fed and nobody was going to attack or kill them (as sometimes happened on the streets). But they were manipulative. When the meal had been served and nothing of it was left, the snack bar staff would cook French fries and burgers. It was at this point the homeless youngsters would arrive, knowing that is what they would get.

This annoyed Fieke. They needed to get good nutritious meals. In one meeting he said, "When one of you says no to them, you all have to say no. You think that if you are polite and nice to them that you will win them for Christ. You will not; they laugh behind your back. I am determined that they will learn that there is another lifestyle. They have to be disciplined. I am going to tell the agency that sponsors them that if they are not on time for the meal that is served then they will get nothing. The agency will then tell them that."

I noticed that as soon as he did that, all the homeless youngsters came in on time for the meal. They did not want to starve and the manipulation of the staff, at least for meals, was over. This was good for our character development. We could see that Fieke poured all his experience of life and walking with the Lord into what he did, and he was training us to do likewise.

---

[15] Song of Solomon 2:15

Sometimes issues needed to be confronted. Ladies working in the hostel were at some degree of risk. Fieke was well aware of this and said to the men, "Gentlemen, you need to look out for the ladies." I took this seriously. When one of our ladies was sitting on a couch with guests, a man sat beside her and took hold of her hand. Her face dropped. She was very uncomfortable with this. I sat down beside the man. My presence put a stop to his behaviour and he let her hand go.

At another meeting Fieke took us through some of the Old Testament and talked about the Passover meal. He had the elements of it and he explained what each one meant. I had never seen anything like it before. There were bitter herbs for pain and suffering, and bread to break for a broken body. It pointed forward to what Christ would do for all mankind on the Cross – but most of the Jews could not see that.

I was most fascinated by one particular piece of bread. With it in his hands, Fieke named the bread, saying that it was this bread that Christ took and broke when he said the following words: "This is my body given for you; do this in remembrance of me." [16] Fieke went on to explain, "None of the disciples would have heard that before, and when the Jews celebrate Passover today, they do not know what to do with this bread."

At the end of the address, he asked if there were any questions. I put my hand up. "That bread is a physical object. You said that the Jews do not know what to do with it, but because it is a physical object, they do not have the option of doing nothing; they must do something with it. So what do they do?"

One of the girls had grown up in Israel. She answered my question. She explained that they hide the bread somewhere in the house and tell the children to go and look for it. The child who finds it gets a prize. I came away from that meeting thinking that if only the Jews could see what that bread represents, then they would see that God has carried out the promise he made to Adam and Eve. A saviour has come and his name is Jesus, and the bread which once

---

[16] Luke 22:19b

pointed forward to his coming is now in remembrance of what he has done on the cross.

The point of staff meetings seemed to be to get all of us thinking and acting as a team, to be single-minded in our goals on how to reach the unbelieving guests. At such a meeting we were confronted with a difficult question. Fieke asked us if we believed that all the guests in the Shelter that night could be saved. There was a long silence. We all knew that in our hearts we did not believe that. I imagined every guest in one night coming to know the Lord as their saviour and I thought it unlikely. One or two perhaps, or even a few, but all of them? It was too much.

At last Fieke broke the silence. "I believe *every* guest in the Shelter tonight could be saved. I do not believe that anyone comes through the front door by accident. God has brought them all here to hear the gospel, and they all get a leaflet explaining how to be saved upon arrival. Some attend the Bible studies, but all of them get something, and when they go home and reflect on their time here, or read the leaflet they got, then one by one I believe that all of them could be saved."

My heart was stirred, for upon hearing it, I believed it too! I did not believe that I was in that place wasting my time. I was doing a work for eternity and what Fieke had said had given me a vision to aim for. *Every guest could be saved.* It was a tremendous thought. Fieke had very gently confronted me with my unbelief and made the prospect of all the guests being saved into something that was achievable, if only we would pray and trust God for it. It would not just be by our efforts. It would be because God was calling the guests to himself.

Being a Christian is not about following rules. It is about having a deep, loving relationship with God. He has done all he can for us. He made us and although we have rebelled against him, he has done everything to win us back. Our sin has been dealt with. God the Father sent Jesus Christ to take on the penalty of our sin by dying on the cross in our place; but because he had no sin, death – the result of sin – had no hold over him. He rose from the dead, and it we trust in him and commit our lives to him then we will be saved. One day we will all rise and those who have trusted him will live with him forever, but for those who have rejected him there will be eternal punishment. It is this that motivated me to go to the Shelter. I wanted to be used of God to inspire others, to win them for Christ and drive others on to further service. Sometimes at the Shelter, when I looked around the streets, it was as if the devil was mocking, saying, "Look what I have done to God's creation." However, I reminded myself that Christ has risen from the dead. The devil has lost, and on the final day he will be cast into hell. What I was doing was not in vain.

21

How Clean is Your House?

The hostel was a hive of activity with lots of people and conversations buzzing around. This was particularly true of the reception area. Every morning there would be a large queue of people getting booked in, asking questions and passing the time of day, and as the day went on, people would wander through reception just talking to friends or the staff.

Once when I was there, I saw a woman enter who looked like she had come straight out of a storybook. Her clothes seemed to be made from a great quantity of lace. She had a very short skirt and jacket, both white, a tiny white hat on her head and white high heel shoes.

"Who is the fairy?" I discreetly asked one of the cleaners.

"Oh, she is one of the prostitutes," she replied. "They often come in here."

The 'fairy' sat down, lit a cigarette and started to talk about small everyday matters with everyone around her. I wondered why she had come in. She was not one of our guests. However she was not propositioning anyone. As she sat and chatted, I realised that I was witnessing her reason for coming in: she just wanted to talk to people in a way that most of us take for granted. She was taking a break and wanted to be accepted as a human being. It was a reminder to me that she was just like all the others in her situation. She knew that at the Shelter she would not be shunned as I am sure she was accustomed to. She would be allowed to sit down and just talk to people. I do not know what became of her, but I hope that was the start of her coming to faith.

I knew that there was another ministry attached to the hostel that did outreach to the prostitutes. I was told that the lady who ran it sometimes came in to pick up her mail. I always imagined her to be young, with a fit, athletic type of figure. One day, however, I saw her and she was nothing like I had imagined. She was a short, stalky older woman. I realised what the girls must have seen in her. To them, she was a mother figure; someone who would keep them safe.

I asked the cleaning supervisor, who seemed to know her, how she set about making contact with the girls. I pointed out that it would be impossible for her to go directly to the girls in the windows as there were men who were pimps who would put a stop to her doing that. The cleaning supervisor said, "She does not go to them; they come to her. They all know who she is and what she does. If they want to get out of the business, they come to her and they know that she will get them out of the city to a safe house." I found that this was true. The prostitutes were familiar with the ministry. I only had to mention the Shelter and they knew the place.

For the sake of safety, we had men on reception in the evenings. On a certain hot night the doors were left open to allow some cool air in. As I stood talking to the man behind the counter, we could see a large number of people passing by. It was clear that they were tourists who had come into the district for the evening just to have a look. They were in a party mood. (One always knew they were only there to look when there were women among them.) Upon seeing this, the man behind the desk seemed to articulate my thoughts. He said, "That really annoys me. They come here to look upon other people's pain." I could not have agreed with him more. I, too, felt the pain in the streets that was such a contrast to the joy found in the Shelter – the joy that one gets from Christ. I felt that the Shelter was like an oasis in a desert of pain and despondency. It was meeting the need of a great thirst that the guests had and also that of the prostitutes who just popped in for a chat.

Guests at the hostel were often people who were travelling, taking in a variety of experiences as they went, finding short term jobs to pay their way. Some were believers, others were not.

Daniel was a cleaner. He was also a believer and he understood suffering as Christians were persecuted in his country. For a couple of days I was ill, and it was Daniel who saw to it that I had the food and drink that I needed to recover. Through his acts of kindness, I experienced brotherly love. I could not help observing that he had suffered so much and yet was not bitter.

He, like all the cleaners, participated in the Bible study programme that was exclusively for them. In this way, unbelievers who were cleaning the hostel heard something from the Bible every day. Some of them were Arabs, and one of the cleaning supervisors who led the Bible studies was himself Arab. He was the right person to discuss biblical truth, for he spoke their language and understood their culture in a way that people like myself could not. On television, in the news, Arabs were depicted as proud people, who did not care for others. However, I found that this was not true. Indeed, many Arabs love people and extend hospitality to others. The hostel provided them with the opportunity to hear about Jesus. Some had come because they knew that they could talk about this in a way that they would not normally be able to. They were seeking the Lord.

22

Appearances can be Deceptive

Every night there was a Bible study to which guests would be invited. I led some of them. One never knew who would come but there were always a few. Some came because they had heard about the Shelter and wanted to ask questions which they had considered in advance. Others were just curious.

It was to one of these studies that a large man came who looked like the gangsters that one sees in Hollywood films. He was clearly a Muslim. At the sight of him, we all felt a sense of dread. The passage was read, some points were made and then the meeting was open for questions. The man was full of questions, but he was not as aggressive as his appearance suggested. He asked many deep, searching questions that made us think. We answered his enquiries as well as we were able.

Then, after some time, one of the girls asked him, "What is it that you want to know?"

His answer pleased and astounded me. He said, "I want to know the truth."

I was accustomed to Westerners who either did not want to hear about Jesus or, if they did, they would not admit to it and would be subtle about how they got information. This man had come to the Shelter to ask his questions.

He went on to say, "Let me tell you something about myself. I have read the Bible and it has given me light. I want to know if it is true."

As he said, "It has given me light," I thought that he was at the same point I had been when the final verses of John's gospel had awakened me to spiritual reality. He already knew it was true, he just wanted to be certain.

We continued the conversation with him for a very long time. I thought that he showed utter determination to know the truth about Jesus. But I never did find out if he came to trust in the Lord or not. Much of the work of the Shelter was like that. One had to be faithful in talking to people, telling them about Jesus and trusting that the Lord would bring them to himself after they had left.

This experience was also a lesson to me. The appearance of the man made us think that he had come to cause trouble, but this was not so. He was sincerely seeking the Lord, and when we are proclaiming the gospel to people, there will be people with all sorts of appearances, some of whom will look terrifying, yet they are the people God is calling.

There was a certain woman. She was no oil painting. She had been a cleaner at the Shelter before I arrived and she popped in to talk to people she knew. I thought she looked awful with her deep wrinkled, shiny skin, bald patches all over her head and raspy voice. She dressed from head to foot in black. I saw one of the Shelter girls give her a hug. The Shelter girl was very beautiful and when I saw them hugging I thought they looked like Beauty and the Beast. I was beginning to learn that appearances can be deceptive. I knew that the Shelter girl was no fool and she would not have hugged that woman if she were dangerous. Indeed it was clear they loved and trusted one another.

I determined in my heart that I was going to get to know the ugly woman. I wanted to know what made her so well loved in spite of her appearance. Her visits were frequent and I found that as I talked to her and got to know her, I loved her too. She was a follower of Jesus. She loved the Lord. I enjoyed her company and looked forward to her visits and what she had to say.

It was decided that we would ask her to tell her life story to all the guests. She agreed to do this in the courtyard where the open windows to the dormitories would mean that not only would she be heard by people sitting in the courtyard but she could also be heard by people who were still in the building. She introduced herself. She came from South Africa and as a child had been experimented on with creams which made her look the way she did. Upon hearing this I felt so much anger that anyone would do such a thing to a child. I knew about apartheid and that there was injustice, but I had never seen this kind of cruelty before, or how some people like that woman had to live with the results of the things that had been done to them.

I thought she looked like a witch when I saw her for the first time. As she gave her life story, I found that evidently other people agreed, as she said that people reacted to her that way. She decided that if she looked like a witch then she *would* be one, and she practised to become a powerful witch and marry the devil. She was successful at casting spells. She could curse people and bad things happened to them. There was, however, one woman she could not curse. She was a Christian who prayed for her and loved her. When she tried to cast a spell on her, it fell back on herself. She hated the woman who loved her with a passion.

The day came when she was on her way to her wedding to marry the devil. The car spun out of control, and on one side of the road was a sheer drop toward which the car was veering. She was sure that the car would go over the drop and she would be killed. So she cried out and said, "Oh God, if you are there, save me!"

She found herself standing in the middle of the road. She had no idea how she had got there, but she was sure God had heard that prayer and answered. For the first time she realised that God is far more powerful than the devil whom she was serving. She sought out the woman who loved and prayed for her and told her what had happened. The woman told her that Christ had died for her and that she should trust him. She showed her that the Bible says, "Submit yourselves, then, to God. Resist the devil, and he will flee from you."[17]

She went on to say that from this verse she had learned to tell the devil to "buzz off", and to her astonishment he did. In all her days as a witch she had never encountered a power like that. God had taken her life and turned it around. On the outside she was ugly, bearing the scars of what had been done to her, but God had saved her and made her beautiful.

When she finished speaking, I was deeply moved. I had never suffered as she had, yet she was not bitter. All her hatred had been replaced by love, and I found that her testimony made me love her all the more. When I was downcast, she could see it and would take me aside, saying that we are all brothers and sisters in Christ and that she wanted to know what troubled me. As I now knew what she had been through, telling her about my own troubles (which seemed a trifle in comparison to hers) was not a problem for me and I appreciated her support.

In my Bible reading I could see that when people trusted in Christ, they were baptised. This was a matter I prayed about. I never raised it with my church as the practice there was one of baptising infants. Moreover, as they were good to me I wanted to remain with them and not go to a Baptist church just because of this one matter. At a staff meeting, Fieke told us that Jim was going to be baptised. Jim was an Englishman who had come to the Shelter as an unbeliever. He had become a cleaner. It was during this time that he trusted in the Lord. Following that, he left the Shelter and went home and then returned as a member of staff. I enjoyed working with him. He had a lot of wisdom gained from his first period at the Shelter. I could not help feeling that I wished that I could also be baptised.

At a later meeting Fieke once again announced that Jim was going to be baptised and that if anyone else wanted to be baptised then we should see Dave about it who would be doing the baptising. I knew this was the answer to my prayer. I had to see Dave and get

---

[17] James 4:7

baptised. Others also wanted to be baptised. In all there were six of us, four men and two women.

It took place in a small chapel only a few streets away from the hostel. As many members of the Shelter staff who could be there attended. We wore white bath robes before going into the water. One by one, we told everyone our life stories about how we had become Christians, before Dave put us under the water. When we came out of the water, a song of our choice would be sung. The baptismal pool was small and we all had to bend our knees as Dave lowered us into the water. It felt so good feeling the water rushing over my face. It seemed that I had lived all my life for that moment. I had chosen a song that I had heard at the Shelter many times – 'Give Thanks with a Grateful Heart' – for indeed I was thankful and grateful to God and to the hostel for the opportunity to be baptised. Fieke preached and said, "Let all the prostitutes and their clients hear that Jesus Christ is Lord." When we had all been baptised and all the singing and preaching done, we went back to the hostel and had a party.

23

Returning Home

My time at the hostel came to an end. Four of the girls tried to persuade me to stay. I was deeply touched by that.

I said to Dave, "I can hardly believe it. When I came here, four of them spoke against me to get rid of me; now four of them have asked me to stay!"

Dave replied, "They judged you too quickly. Now they have got to know you."

I attended my final meeting at The Cleft. I was given the opportunity to address everyone and say goodbye to them. Some come forward to pray for me. The first person to come down the passageway to do so was Edwin. He was one of the homeless young people whom I had met at the Shelter. He had always gone out of his way to be helpful to us, as though he was trying to prove to everyone that he was a good guy. Edwin seemed to appreciate the love shown to him, and God convicted him of his sin. Edwin had disappeared from the Shelter and we later found out that he had felt such a burden of guilt for the crimes that he had committed that he had gone to the police and confessed. He was jailed and then returned to the Shelter with a prison crew cut hairstyle. Now here was that same man praying for me. I was overwhelmed by the change that I saw in him and his care for me.

Fieke had said that he would only have us for a short time and that during that time he wanted us to learn more of Christ and how to communicate the gospel to others. It was a way of saying that he was not only concerned for the present but looked to the future and how God would use us, and he was very conscious that God was using him to train us and that it was his responsibility to do it well. He succeeded to do that in me, I believe. I experienced things that made me grow in my knowledge and love of the Lord. I discovered the truth of the scripture that says, "And we know that in all things God works for the good of those who love him, who have been called according to his purpose,"[18] for I experienced it.

It had been an intense school of learning but in the end I loved it and thanked the Lord for it. On the day I left, some of the staff and guests came with me to the airport to see me off. I boarded the plane, and as I looked out of the window as the plane rose, I could not help thinking of all the people I had met and grown to love and was now leaving behind.

Upon my return, I had to register as unemployed again. Going to the unemployment office every two weeks was demeaning. One never gets used to it. It is always a dreadful experience. I decided to bring that to a swift end by entering a government scheme whereby I would still get benefit plus a little more while doing some office training. It was like going back to school but now I was in my thirties. Most of the people on the training scheme were school leavers. However, there was a sufficient number of mature adults to make the atmosphere more comfortable. The school leavers were in a difficult position. They had not been able to get jobs so they entered the training scheme to get money – it was not because their heart's desire was to be office workers. Moreover, they still behaved as though they were still at school, having only recently left.

One of the adults training with me was the same man that I had first met some years prior when I was doing a summer outreach

[18] Romans 8:28

with Youth With A Mission – the one who had been asked to leave the team with no explanation. I decided that as we were going to be on the scheme for a year, it would not be wise for me to ask him why he had been dismissed from the team. Once again I saw all the signs in him that had disturbed me, but I did my best to get on with him.

Sometimes he told dirty stories to the young girls about himself. I found this embarrassing as I knew that he was attending a church and that his daily conduct was not in keeping with this. The worst day came when he told all of the girls around me an unsavoury story about me. He had just made it up on the spot because he thought it was funny. All the girls turned round and looked at me. I could see the shock on their faces. After a silence that seemed to go on forever, one of them asked me if it was true. I just sat there glaring at him. I did not know what to say; she had a smirk on her face. I was so angry. At last I decided that my silence spoke volumes. I did not answer the question. This had the desired effect. It was clear to the girls that he had lied, and I am sure my displeasure was equally clear to him.

I was to suffer further embarrassment from him when someone asked him what he had done at the weekend and he said, "Believe it or not, I went to church." His entire lifestyle did not convey that of being a Christian. I often wondered when his church was going to do something to discipline him. I thought that he was a prime example of people who know the facts of the gospel but do not make it their own. I was reminded of the Bible passage that says, "You believe that there is one God. Good! Even the demons believe that – and shudder."[19] Such people have deceived themselves into thinking they are saved, when in fact nothing could be further from the truth, and unless they turn from their wicked ways and truly follow the Lord they will enter into eternal damnation.[20]

I thought back to the days of attending the Ranch Bible studies. Richard would often say, "If I go to McDonald's, that does

---

[19] James 2:19
[20] See Matthew 7:21-23

not make me a hamburger, so likewise going to church does not make you a Christian." I once saw an evangelist stand by a chair and say, "I can say that I trust this chair to take my weight, but unless I actually get on the chair then I do not really trust." Likewise, unless we, in our hearts, totally submit to Jesus Christ then we are not truly saved.

24

Encounters

I have discovered that the devil is cunning and often attacks, when least expected and from a place that one would not think of. Sometimes it starts with an everyday, innocent thing.

While unemployed it was good to get out of the house even if it was only to walk around a town centre or walk in the park. It was while looking in shop windows that I met Tanya. I had known her as a child when she had attended that first YWAM Summer of Service that I had been a part of. She had been a child then, and now she was in her late teens.

She smiled at me and we got talking. We walked around the town centre looking at the shop displays. She was very enjoyable company. Her father had made a profession of faith some years before. We kept walking and talking, and when we came to her house I was invited in. There was no one else there. She made coffee and we sat talking.

She became very emotional as she talked about her life. Her parents had separated and this had had a profound effect upon her. She said that she had felt depressed when she went out that morning, but now she was a different person inside. She felt better. I was really moved and I hugged her. As we embraced, emotions took over and we kissed.

We continued to talk and after a while she said, "I am still a virgin." She said it in a tone that sounded like she was pleading a case with me, to persuade me to go to bed with her. It was very tempting and I was flattered. I have the same desires as any other human being. Who would know about it? It would be our secret. However, just like a loving parent who sees danger, the Holy Spirit within me restrained me. I made my excuses and left the house quickly.

I reflected on those passages of the Bible about dying to self. Sometimes it is not good to give in to our own desires for they are sinful and it is a day by day battle. Sometimes a legitimate desire is wrong because the circumstances are wrong and we have to please God by putting him first. By doing this, we demonstrate that we are truly children of God and are adopted into his family. We became part of the family when we truly believe in Christ and submit to him.

As I looked back on this incident, I realised that my whole ministry could have been ruined by a foolish act. It is true that our adversary the devil walks about like a roaring lion seeking whom he may devour. I also know that Jesus prays to the Father for me and I am convinced that it is this that stopped me that day. As I read the Bible I see the temptations Jesus resisted, and we are told that after this the devil left him until a more opportune time. I often find that the devil does indeed leave me until another time and I know that for as long as I am in this mortal body there will be other battles to fight. I need to be on guard.

I had continued studying with the Open University and my efforts met with success. Every year I had passed the coursework and exams, and finally I graduated. I was now ready to apply to be a candidate for the ministry of the Church of Scotland. I realised that this would present difficulty but I was ready for it. It was the mid-1990s. In my mind, I could see how I would present myself in the best possible way to be an acceptable candidate for the ministry. I had no illusions about the challenge.

However, God sometimes acts in unexpected ways. This was to be one of them. I sent a letter to the Church of Scotland Head

Office in Edinburgh requesting an application form. The reply I got surprised me. It was not the form that I expected but a letter from my former minister. In it he wrote that he would like to have a meeting with me at his home. I knew he worked in the Head Office – he had left the church to go there – but it had not occurred to me that my letter would end up on his desk.

I went to see him and he voiced some concerns. He said that he thought that I had a remarkable teaching gift but he wondered if I would be any good as a pastor. He said that he thought there was a barrier between me and other people. He found this difficult to say and it took a lot of courage. To enter the ministry, I would need to have him as a referee, and while he was willing to do this, it was not without reservations that he would have to express. I understood what he was saying but I had never felt that way on the Scripture Union, Youth With A Mission, London City Mission or Shelter teams that I had served on. The barrier was just in my local church and he had never seen me in those other situations. He left me to make my decision.

I still felt from reading Timothy that I had something to offer to the building of God's kingdom. As I had discovered I had a teaching gift, it seemed logical that I should be a minister. However, without unreserved support that would not happen. At the interviews they would be looking for someone slick; I had planned on how to be slick, but reservations on a reference would be damaging.

After some thought I decided to change my plan. Instead I decided to apply for missions. The meeting I had with my former minister was God-ordained. It caused me to rethink. I have often thought that if I had applied to the Church of Scotland, I would have been successful but would not be where I am now with a worldwide view of mission. I would be in local church where my vision would be only for local issues, or certainly no further than Scotland, so I have no regrets about that meeting nor the decision that I made.

I thought that if I were to go into missions then I should go into one that I already knew a great deal about. In the past I had begun two applications for Operation Mobilisation – and then changed my mind as I realised that I was not suitable for the fields that I was considering. I knew the Wycliffe Bible Translators but because of my bad experience with languages at university I did not think I would be any good to them. I wrote to the Shelter and asked if I could rejoin the staff for six months. They replied by saying that, after much prayer, they felt that the season for me at the Shelter was over. I was not surprised at this. I was only testing them; I knew they were right.

I was in receipt of the Operation Mobilisation monthly newsletter. In one of the letters was a prayer request for people to join the Operation Mobilisation United Kingdom team. I prayed for other people to go and join the team, but I had no thoughts of going myself as I knew very little about OM. However, the following month the letter came again and it had the same request, but this time it had details of the jobs. When I read the details, I thought, "I could do that!" And so... I applied.

25

A Very Long Day

A date for my interviews was fixed. I had to travel to Shropshire, but during the period that I had to go there, the railway was having intermittent one-day strikes. I did not want to find that they were on strike on the day that I needed to travel so I informed OM by phone that I would come by coach. The woman I spoke to said that she would be at the coach station to meet me upon arrival. But when I got to Wrexham, the woman was not there.

I was in a town that I had never been to before, but at least I had a phone number for OM. I went into a phone box and dialled the number. As I did so, a bearded man appeared outside the phone box, waiting his turn. OM said that they would call me back soon and asked for my number. So I stepped back out of the box and the bearded man went in. I asked him if he would be long as I was expecting a return phone call. He said he would be quick and closed the door. He then stuck his head out the door and said, "You are not George Falconer, by any chance, are you?" I said I was. He then introduced himself, shook my hand and told me that he had been sent to meet me.

He drove me to the village. It was dark and there seemed to be far more roundabouts on the road than I had ever seen before. We pulled up at a house and I was introduced to the couple I would be staying with for the night. Over breakfast I spoke to them both. The husband told me that he was the administration manager and his wife was in the same department. They took me to the office. I silently prayed, "Oh God, you know how negative I feel about having backed out of other missions and being turned down by others. This is the last time I shall do this. If they say no, I will never apply for missions again." This was not fanciful thinking; it was a firm decision.

The couple took me to the office and I was shown into the team meeting room where morning devotions were taking place. The team sat round the room and I observed people as they entered. In the corner sat an Asian man. He led the meeting. He gave a short address from scripture and there was prayer before everyone went to their offices to start work. I was shown to the Personnel Department for the longest interview that I had ever had. Details of your life come up in a way that in the secular world they would not. During the course of the interview I gave my life story. I was then interviewed by the man whose house I had spent the night in, and then by the field leader. At the end of the process the receptionist called me and said they would like me to go back to Personnel.

"Oh no," I thought. "What has gone wrong this time?"

I felt apprehensive as I went up the stairs. I sat in a chair in front of the personnel officer, waiting for the bad news that I thought was going to come. I was expecting a rejection and prepared my heart for it.

However, she asked a question: "What do you think you would find most difficult in OM?"

I remained silent while I thought about the question. Then I said, "Living by faith." By this I meant that I understood that in OM there is no visible means of financial support. I knew that the money had to come from church, friends and family for me to live. This would be a major step of faith. There was no product or service to sell.

She replied, "We think we can make you an offer."

I was surprised and shocked. I felt like I was going to fall off the chair.

She could see this and asked, "What is wrong?"

"Nothing," I replied. "I just thought you would want to think about it for a couple of days."

"We do not believe in waiting when we think we have the right person," she said.

On my way home I was jubilant. I could not have been happier. I was going to join OM, one of the biggest mission societies in the world, and the strange thing was that up until then, OM was the one that I had had the least amount of contact with. My world was about to change.

A couple who were the OM representatives in Scotland came to visit the prayer meeting in my church to let us see the work of OM that I would be joining. The church had very little experience of world mission and OM was not well known to them. I really appreciated that they wanted to come to my church and introduce the organisation. I felt deeply touched. The couple were called Arthur and Wilma, and from that day on I became friends with them. It was the first time that I had met OM regional representatives. They were working on their own in the OM Scottish office making people and churches aware of OM and keeping them up-to-date with the latest news. My church was new to them. They had photographs and literature, and they encouraged those at the prayer meeting to pray for me as I joined.

I started making plans for my new life in OM. It was, however, delayed for a few months. Raising money for it was a challenge, and when I saw an opportunity to get some, I took it. Rosyth Naval base was being run down and they needed people in the interim. Many had already left to take up longer-term jobs. This had created some short-term jobs at the base, and one of them was offered to me. I was already familiar with the base as when I was unemployed and doing office training, I had been sent on placement to one of the catering companies there. I therefore knew what the inside of the place looked like. The team I joined were responsible for the care of the buildings. Any work that needed to be done went through our office. I thought that this was good for me as it got me into regular work before joining the OM team. It was office work, and I would be doing that when I joined OM, so I looked upon my time with the Ministry of Defence as further office training. I saved as much money as I could to get me started in OM and finally the day came when I handed in my notice. I was ready to go.

26

Getting Started

I was afraid that the same thing would happen at the start of my OM days as had happened at the Shelter. God answered this prayer – it did not happen – but I realised that I had brought my previous hurt and fear into the new situation. After prayer I felt much more confident.

Operation Mobilisation encouraged everyone joining to participate in one of their short-term programmes prior to joining so that applicants had a little experience of OM. It was not compulsory, and I decided not to do that as I thought that I already had a good deal of mission experience from the Shelter. There I had met and worked with people from all over the world and OM was going to be similar. I had also served on my own church's Scripture Union teams; this had taught me the value of the church and that the missions organisation is simply a tool for the church to use.

All of us had to go to a training conference in the Netherlands. I had to travel to London and board a coach that OM had hired for all the British applicants going to the conference. We travelled during the night. At the stroke of midnight the personnel officer said, "It is past midnight; you are now all OM-ers. Well done!" Thus the morning of my new life had started. It was January 9th, in the mid-1990s. My kaleidoscope life seemed to shine like the sun, even although it was evening and dark as pitch.

The crossing on the ferry was smooth and we stopped for breakfast at the OM base in Belgium. Before we entered the base, the personnel officer warned us, "They will try to recruit you. Just remember, you are all spoken for." At breakfast we found out that she was right. The Belgium team did try to recruit us, but it was largely in vain as all of us were allocated to fields in advance, except for one man, and even he did not join them; he decided to go to one of the ships which OM had called Logos 2.

We were told that a disabled man was driving to the conference and on the way he would be picking up passengers at an airport. It was requested that one of us remained behind to go with the man to the airport as it was not possible for him to go into the terminal to meet the passengers. He needed someone else to do that. I volunteered to help. I thought that as my aunt was disabled, I was probably the best qualified person to do this. The man introduced himself as Jonathan. I got in his van and off we went to the airport. I did as I had agreed by going into the terminal to meet the passengers. Jonathan was a very influential leader. One of the passengers I met was the leader of the work in Sweden. Thus I started meeting men who were big influencers in world mission on my very first day.

Jonathan then took us to the conference centre. When we arrived, I found that I was sharing a room with two Englishmen who were joining the Asia Challenge teams. At the end of each day it was good to talk to them and share our experiences. We were learning together and bonding.

Every day we attended sessions. OM works in many countries, so one of the things that has to be discussed is culture shock. I had first seen this in Dennis in my school days and I had experienced it at the Shelter. It was made very clear to us that our way of doing things is not necessarily the only way of doing things. Other cultures do things differently and have to be valued in the same way that we value our own. Having met people at the Shelter from the Arab world and other parts of Europe, I had a good insight into this. I had come to appreciate that the Dutch deal with problems by confronting them head on, and it worked. Each culture has a world view, and many of them put themselves at the centre of it. This is certainly true of the British.

There were sessions teaching about the four personality types. Some people are detailers. They make good accountants. If any detail is out of place, they will spot it. Others get things done and they will press ahead with completing tasks at the cost of hurting others, even if they do not mean to do so. Some people are more empathetic. They feel things and they get alongside other people to comfort them. The final types were the visionaries. They have a very broad view of where we need to get to. All the personality types need each other. The broad view people need the detailers. Those who get things done need those who are more empathetic. This is biblical. Scripture teaches us to value one another.[21]

A counselling service was made available to all of us in case we thought that there were issues affecting our lives that we would like to talk through. I never felt the need to make use of it myself because I had spent so much time being counselled in my own church, long before joining OM, that any issues I may have had had been dealt with. However, many people do come with issues hanging over them and being at the conference provided the opportunity to bring them to the surface.

Jonathan led one of the sessions. He said that he had joined OM for the summer programme – and here he was thirty years later, still on the programme! I saw in him a life of service to God in the face of difficulty. He had been disabled in a motorbike accident that had put him in a wheelchair, but this had not in any way diminished his love for the Lord. Indeed, he was one of the OM leaders and an inspiration to others.

It was exciting to meet people from all over the world going into mission. I felt that I had become part of something so much bigger than myself. There were some that I regret not keeping in contact with. One such man introduced himself to me saying, "I am

---

[21] 1 Corinthians 12:21-25

a Red Indian, George. The woo-woo-woo kind." As he said this, he put his hand to his mouth and made the sound that you hear in Hollywood Western movies when the Indians are attacking the waggon train. He was what we now call a Native American. Reaching them is difficult and so I knew that people such as he were very rare; I count myself privileged to have met such a man.

At the end of each day, we would relax with French fries and mayonnaise. One day an English woman whom I had not met before walked up to me and took some of mine. Her eyes seemed to give a naughty smile as she ate them. I could not believe that someone would do that. This marked the start of a friendship. While I had been at the Ministry of Defence, Susan had left the OM ship called Doulos and become part of the Operation Mobilisation United Kingdom Personnel Department. I enjoyed her company and I could laugh with her a great deal.

I also met a number of other people who would be working in the same office as I would. I had not realised that I would be joining with several computer programmers, from the USA. A new computer system had been created and these young men were going to commission it. It had been a long time in the planning.

There was a session led by a man who was an evangelist in a Western country. He told us that he always got people lost. This introduction grabbed our attention. He pointed out that people had no sense that they are lost and that God will one day judge them. They need to know that they are lost *now*, before it is too late, so that they can turn to Christ. To do this, he needed to *get them lost*. By this he meant that he had to make them aware of the fact that they are lost. He did this by presenting us with an imaginary situation in which he was on a plane sitting next to a man called Sean. He would get talking to him. Sean thinks that he is okay. He has little to worry about. Life is good. Sean thinks he is not perfect but he is not a sinner. He does no one any harm, in fact, where he has the opportunity, he does good deeds for other people and he hopes that if there is a God then God will be pleased with him.

"Have you kept the Ten Commandments?" the man asks.
"I think I have," says Sean.

"OK, Sean, let us see how many of them you have kept. I have a Bible here. Let us look at them." The man opens the Bible to Exodus 20:2-17. "So tell me, Sean, the first Commandment tells you to have no other gods, have you done that? Do you worship the living God and him alone?"

Looking somewhat taken aback, Sean says, "Well... ahem... no. I tend to not think about him, and I am not that bothered."

"Well, Sean," says the man, "have you ever read a horoscope?"

"Yes," says Sean. "It is only a bit of fun. Nobody takes it seriously."

"Oh, but God takes it seriously, Sean," says the man. "Unless you are worshipping him with all your heart and soul then you have other gods, even if they exist only in your mind. Well, never mind, we can see you have broken the first Commandment but there are still nine to go. Let's see if you do any better with the second."

And he works through all Ten Commandments in the same way.

Finally he says, "You have broken all the Commandments. So, Sean, if you have not been able to keep the Commandments up until now, even if you started to, you would still be guilty of having broken them. That means you are lost, Sean. You are a sinner. Do you agree?"

By telling us this imaginary story, the presenter was demonstrating what he actually did. He met people and used the Ten Commandments to prove that they are not the good, nice people they think they are. Most people do not understand that, and this was his way of making them see it. This is in fact what the Commandments are for. They are there to help people see that they cannot keep them, for our nature is to sin. We cannot help ourselves.

My life was changing. It was exciting and terrifying at the same time. None of us had a visible income. We depended on friends and churches to finance us. It seemed strange, but I knew that some people lived like this. God had set them apart to do the work that they do. I was entering their number. I felt like a tightrope walker over the Grand Canyon. You know the rope is safe but you dare not look down. The New Recruits Conference was the start of a new life. It had been great, but the time soon came for us to depart to our fields.

On the way to the Netherlands the ferry crossing had been smooth. This was not the case on the way back. It was a stormy night and the ship rolled. I do not travel well by sea and soon I started to feel very ill. I had been advised that if I ever felt that way I should lie on the floor and soon I would feel better. I found this to be true and so I completed most of the return voyage flat on my back. When we reached the port, we boarded the coach. There was a black girl whom I had seen on the ferry. She had been just as ill as I had been. I also knew that she had committed to serving two years on the OM ship Logos 2 which was in Belfast at the time, and all those joining had to sail to Belfast from the Scottish port town of Stranraer. As I am a Scot, she realised that I was likely to know something about Stranraer. She looked at me across the passageway and asked, "What is Stranraer?" I realised that she did not mean the town. She was thinking about how ill she had been on the ferry and she had committed herself to two years on a ship, and if Stranraer was what she thought it was then perhaps she was going to be just as ill again. I confirmed her worst fears. "It's a ferry," I said. I saw her eyes roll and she settled back in her seat.

We all got off the coach in London, and those of us going to the OM UK office boarded a minibus for the last leg of the journey. We arrived at night, and in the darkness as we entered the site, the driveway to the office and the houses seemed to be very long. My body ached for bed. I was shown to the flat I would be living in and a German was shown to the same flat. We were to be flat mates with someone else whom we had not yet met but who clearly already lived there. I went to bed, to get ready for Day One of my new life.

27

The Welcoming

On that first January morning, I formally met the team. Some mornings started with times of devotion. I was loving it! There were two young women whom I had met at the training conference who were joining the team. One was new to the organisation, the other was Susan, who had helped herself to my French fries at the conference. Both of them were joining the Personnel Department. The others were the computer programmers. I discovered that the man I had met when being interviewed, and in whose house I had stayed, was the head of the department that I would be joining. This process of meeting people, and also learning about the health and safety aspects of the office, was called Orientation. I realised that in joining the team, it was not like going to work in any other office. This was not just a job; it was spiritual work. The Bible warns us that we have an enemy. He is the devil and he will try to upset the work and us if he has the chance. God constrains him, but he is very real. I had no illusions. This would not be like joining the civil service.

The computer programmers quickly discovered that missions are very different to the commercial world. There was no software package available that met all of the office needs and so they had to create their own. The original plan was that it would take six months. As more obstacles occurred it took more time and eventually went live after a period of seven years. From this I learned that God does provide and he carries out his plans, but our timescale is not always his. The Apostle Paul sometimes made plans and had to change them, yet the Bible makes it clear that he was led by the Holy Spirit, and so it is the same today. We are led by God's Holy Spirit, but as he interacts with human beings so plans may change. The programmers were people that had been prayed into the work. Only one of them had met the team before and they quickly became a team in their own right, not only in terms of the work, but also for the people they were. I enjoyed the company of every one of them and we had the shared experience of joining OM together.

My desk was in Reception, opposite a lady who had been in the organisation for a very long time. Aileen became like a mentor to me. I thought that she had a mind like an encyclopaedia. She seemed to know every aspect of the organisation and the people in it. As I would be sending out the mail, I realised that this would be vital knowledge for me as I would be sending it to the people and places that she talked about. She was also very good at making suggestions about how things could be done just as efficiently but at a lower cost. I valued her friendship. Her husband was retired and they had season tickets for the local amateur theatre. The postman who brought our delivery every morning was a member too, so when he arrived, he and Aileen would talk about the theatre's latest production. She asked me if I would like to come with her and her husband to see one of the plays. I accepted, and I loved it so much that I joined the theatre.

I could see that I was now part of a vast organisation. God had brought it into existence in a very simple way. George Verwer, an American, had become a Christian when he was seventeen years old. He went to Moody Bible College and, while there, he and a couple of friends went on a short term mission to Mexico. This was the first mission that gave birth to Operation Mobilisation. The following year they did the same thing, but more people joined them, and then the year after that, once again even more people joined them. It grew year by year into an international organisation.

We seek to make Christ known to everyone. Getting to know how it worked and the people in it would take time. In my mind I could see myself sitting at the desk, knowing very little. I made a decision. I decided that I would have just one aim for a year and that would be what I called "getting my legs under the desk". I would get on with the job, learn it well, get to know the people and let them get to know me. I would not try to do other things before I was ready. This proved to be a wise decision.

One by one, I met the team who had worked in the office for some time. One of the men asked me one evening if I would like to come and meet one of the families. I accepted, and when I entered their home it was a whole new experience. I had grown up in a large town where most people were married to someone else who also came from the same town or from the surrounding district. In a missions organisation people from other parts of the world meet, and my hosts had met on the OM ship Doulos. Colin and Bo had been married for a number of years and had children. He was an Englishman and she was from South Korea. I was to learn that the South Korean church is very large indeed. He was doing everything he could to embrace his wife's culture. I thought that it was lovely to see a man showing such devotion to his wife. I enjoyed their company in the years to come, but that first meeting seeing an Englishman and Korean as a married couple was a visual illustration to me that I had entered a new and very different world to the one that I was accustomed to.

When I was studying for my degree, the opportunity had arisen to do Information Technology. This made me familiar with using a computer. I discovered, from my first day in the office, that God must have planned this for me, because the experience I had made the job a little easier to learn; particularly regarding databases, as I had studied them for my degree. I had also become good at touch typing. There was another lady in Reception with Aileen and me. Tina was the receptionist. She was not quite full time and I had to fill in the hours when she was not there. I had done reception work as part of my office training so once again I saw how God had led me. He had given me training to do this job, even when I did not realise it. Filling in at Reception meant that I not only took calls from supporters calling in, but also from the other offices and representatives around the country. I got to know a lot of people as voices on the phone before I met them face to face. My plan for getting my legs under the desk was working.

I had to learn to use the automatic mailer. I had never seen a machine like it. It was a time-saving device. Letters went in at one end and envelopes in the other. The machine folded the letters and put them in the envelopes at rapid speed. I learned how to take addresses from the database, send them to the printer and put the letters through it to have the addresses printed on the envelope. Sometimes I would reflect on how I came into the organisation. It was by receiving those letters that I joined and here I was sending out the same letters. I was now God's instrument being used to send those letters to other men and women who were also being called to serve God in missions just as I was doing.

We bonded together well as a group and as friends, and were in and out of each other's houses eating and talking together. I largely enjoyed this. However, it did have its downside. I sometimes would go out to a church meeting at night and come home to find that one of my flatmates had a visitor – usually someone else from the team – whom I was not expecting to see sitting on our couch! I had just come back and felt very tired, but I was not able to go to bed due to the unexpected visitor. I felt like I was living in a hotel with no home. I did not want to alienate anyone or be offensive.

One of my flatmates was Fritz. He came from Germany. One of the issues that arose was whether we would share the cooking or do it ourselves. Peter, the third man in the flat, was not there a great deal, and we also realised that cooking can be very culture-specific. So we agreed to cook our own meals. I assumed that at twenty-six Fritz would know something about cooking – but I was wrong! He treated it like a survival exercise!

He asked questions such as, "How do you know when meat is cooked?"

I explained, "If it looks cooked and you can easily stick a fork in it, then it is cooked."

Fritz was still not confident. He bought a microwave, and for the nine months he was with us, he lived on microwave meals. I had assumed that everyone could cook if they made the effort. When I was being interviewed, I was asked if I could cook and I had thought that question had come up for everyone, including those coming from abroad. Evidently it had not.

Another question from Fritz illustrated to me that food can be cultural. He asked, "Do all the British eat as much fish as you do?"

"When you come from a nation that is surrounded by the sea, you eat what is in it," I replied.

"In Germany we think fish is a luxury," said Fritz. "We only eat it about once a month." I have no idea if this is true as Fritz had told me when I met him that he was not a typical German.

Fritz was also unprepared for the weather. We had both joined the team in January and he frequently complained about being cold. I think that it was the damp air that we have in the UK that affected him most. No amount of heat from the radiator was enough for him. Many of his conversations started with the words, "In Germany..." The culture shock hit him harder than he had anticipated. He knew the British would be different, but the differences were greater than he had imagined.

We did not have a television in the flat. There was a television lounge on the ground floor and sometimes this meant men would come into it carrying the food they had prepared. I could see they had the same problem that Fritz had; a lot of it seemed to be almost raw. Nevertheless they ate it.

A man from South Africa joined the team. He was a brilliant cook. He looked at this and said to me, "I see the things they eat. Could you and I cook for them?"

I said, "If you cook for them, they will never learn. Necessity is the mother of invention."

He took it upon himself to cook for them anyway. In this way, they all survived for a couple of years.

I had not planned on joining OM when I went to university; God led me into it much later. There are some people who are the opposite. They are really focussed and they plan their lives in detail.

Keith was such a man. I was getting on with my job in the mailroom when he walked in to get some literature which was on shelves in the room. I was using the automatic mailer and I paused when I saw him. We had never spoken before. He told me he was from the USA and was a programmer working on the project that all the other men who had arrived with me were working on. He had a passion for mission and had always had some sort of project that he was working on at any given time. He told me that he had always planned ahead and carried out his plans. He was a visionary – a person who could see what needed to be done to achieve an objective – and he was doing his part in it. I could see that Keith was the opposite of me. I did not plan things the way he did and neither of us were right or wrong, we were just different. We became good friends. I appreciated his sense of vision and his intelligence. Above all he deeply loved God and had a very good understanding of the Bible. When the opportunity arose he loved to stand in front of the team, open the Bible and teach from it. His life reflected what he taught. In this respect, Keith and I were likeminded.

Another friend was Katie. She was a little woman from Barbados who had served on the OM ship Logos and had been on board when it had run aground. I also formed a friendship with Alex who also came from Barbados and from the same church as Katie. One day in conversation I called Katie "black". She started to laugh and laugh and laugh. I wondered if she was ever going to be able to stop.

At long last she said, "George, back home, I am not thought of as black."

"But you *are* black, Katie," I insisted, "and there is nothing wrong with being black."

This set her off laughing again. She did not explain what was funny. I could see that her skin was paler than most black people, but she was in my mind undeniably black.

I related this incident to Alex, who also came from Barbados. He said, "In Barbados, every now and then, a child is born like Katie. We have a history of slave masters from the UK, and their genes are in the population; sometimes it shows when a child has skin that is paler than most of the population."

I loved both of them. I did not care what colour they were. It was, however, an early experience of cultural differences on an OM team.

My Dunfermline church had been my spiritual home. I now needed to find a new one. I cast my mind back to my university days when David, my block warden, had said that when you are looking for a new church, the closest Bible-believing one to your home is the one. I had noticed that the village had more than one church, so I asked one of the team about the nearest one. Then, on my first Sunday in England, I visited one of the churches and got talking to the vicar. I broached the subject of the other churches and, in particular, the one that I wanted to know about.

Armed with this information, the following Sunday I went there. I saw a woman and a boy, and judging by the manner in which she spoke to him, I thought that she was one of two things: either a teacher or his mother. She proved to be the latter. She was also the pastor's wife. There was another family, another man slightly younger than I, a lady and an elderly gentleman. It was the smallest church I had ever seen. However, from what I knew about them that I had learned from the vicar of the other church, I thought that I would fit in well. I found that I was right about that. I grew very close to the pastor and his wife, and to the elderly man.

I was asked if I would like to join the church. I wondered how this was possible as I was still a member of my church in Dunfermline and I was not aware that sometimes one can be a member of two churches. The constitution of this church permitted that. I thought that if I were a member, I would be in a position to play a much more active part. So I agreed to join, but I needed the approval of all the members. We were at the pastor's house when I was asked if I would give my testimony. They wanted to be sure that they admitted a true believer and not just someone who was very religious, or who only believed the facts of the gospel but had never truly trusted in Christ. I told them the story of how I had received the Gideon's Bible at school and the effect it had on me. I told how later I had met Richard who told me that salvation was a free gift and all I had to do was accept Christ and to trust in him to save me from sin. Then I was asked to leave the room while everyone else discussed the situation. After several minutes, I was invited back into the room and they congratulated me on becoming a member of the church. It was as simple as that.

In a small church there is nowhere to hide. Everyone is very visible and plays an active part. I was asked to be treasurer and with some trepidation I accepted. However, I quickly discovered that being treasurer was not my gifting, so I gave it up and became secretary, which I enjoyed very much. The church was governed by the congregation. It was independent and there was no hierarchy. I really enjoyed the meetings, including the business ones. I had found my new spiritual home.

I still did not feel at home when I went back to the flat. I felt like I was living in a hotel with no control over my surroundings. When people, whom I lived with, left the team, new people would move in and I had no say on who lived with me. I lived in a constant state of slight depression. No matter how well I got on with the people I lived with, I was haunted by the feeling of helplessness. I considered that people who live what we call 'normal lives' did not put up with this. Somehow, living with flatmates, no matter how much I respected them, was not fun. One of them had a very loud snore that penetrated the bedroom wall, making sleep difficult. I used to put the radio on and wear headphones as this drowned out the snoring and I would get to sleep.

The feeling of having no sense of control over my home environment did not abate. After about a year and a half I decided that I needed to do something about it. At least I needed to *talk* about it. I went to see the field leader, and I told him how I felt and why. At first he indicated that he could not do anything about it, but at a second meeting that followed shortly, he told me that he and his wife were going to move out of their house and it would be divided into two flats. I could have one of them. This was just what I needed. As the weeks went by, I saw the conversion work taking place. I looked forward in anticipation to having my own home. At last the day came when it was complete and I moved in. I felt so much better. Life was good, and I think that everyone around me noticed that I was more upbeat.

28

Reaching the World

In those early years, I was very privileged to meet people who, unlike me, had not just joined the organisation after all the hard work of setting it up had been done by other people. Our field leader was one of those people. He had joined the ship ministry before there was a ship and was part of the team that bought the Logos, the very first ship. Another of those people was Cyril. He came from Liverpool and when I joined, Cyril was still organising fundraising dinners for the ship ministry. He had been a marine engineer and he was the first Chief Electrician on the Logos. Periodically Cyril would visit the office and take literature away with him that he could distribute at fundraisers. I still greatly admire people like Cyril who get a work started. They are the modern day mission pioneers whom God has brought to the fore to do the work. I also met other people who had been there in the early days of the ship ministry.

As the months went by, and I listened to the things that they had to say, I could see that there was often a demand for certificated officers. I was learning the truth of the scripture that says, "The harvest is plentiful, but the labourers are few. Pray you therefore the lord of the harvest to send workers into the field."[22] In missions there is always a need for more workers in any mission field, so at the prayer meetings we would ask the Lord to give us more workers and often this would be for specific tasks. They had prayed for a mailroom manager and I was the answer to their prayers.

I was also privileged to return to the Netherlands for an international gathering where the speaker was Joni Erickson Tada. I had read her books and seen the film about her life. When she was seventeen years old, she broke her neck in a diving accident. She started a ministry aimed at the disabled. The subject she spoke to us on was 'Suffering'. It was lovely to meet her husband, who does so much to look after her. She called an extra meeting for those of us who had disabled friends and relatives so that we could talk about them and pray for them. I attended this meeting to talk about my mother's twin sister who was partially paralysed by polio.

I firmly believe that Jesus Christ should be made known to all of mankind, and the task of doing that starts with prayer. I had learned about prayer in Dunfermline, and in OM we had prayer meetings in which we prayed for the OM work throughout the world. My part in that was to send out the prayer letters to help other Christians pray for the work, support it and join it.

In my younger days I had attended a Keith Green memorial concert in Edinburgh. He had been a Christian singer-songwriter with a passion for mission, but he died at the age of twenty-eight. The memorial concerts followed. I had bought one of his albums at the concert and put other leaflets I picked up that night in the album sleeve. I know the date of the concert. I did not realise at the time but I had picked up the leaflets from an OM stand. This was another link in the chain that brought me into OM. From that time until the day I joined was sixteen years, so I say to those who recruit that sometimes it take a long time! It took sixteen years to recruit me.

Many people join OM with a variety of skills. They are perfect for the places that they go to and I have a part in supporting them. Thus the work that I do makes an impact on the whole world.

---

[22] Matthew 9:37

I think that the twelve disciples who followed Jesus were just like a missions organisation. There were all sorts of people in it and somehow they had to get along in spite of personality differences. For most people, going to church means that if there is anyone you have difficulty getting along with, you can avoid the issue as you only meet for an hour once or twice a week. Apart from that, you have no need to have anything to do with each other. In a missions organisation we see each other every day and we have Jesus' instruction to love one another as he loved us.[23] This is a command, not optional, but loving one another does not come naturally; it is something that needs to be worked at. Christ loved in a sacrificial way and we are to love and support one another. While still flat-sharing, I had a flatmate whom I found difficult to get on with and it was clear that he had some personal issues. I also had my own issue, namely, my lack of a sense of home.

Jesus had to deal with personal conflict among the disciples. This is normal. Jesus had to deal with James and John who were brothers, and their mother who wanted to see her sons get the top seats in heaven. In our day it is no different. The details may change but the core problem is what remains of our sinful nature, and I found that I had to battle with mine. Some people challenge us more than others.

In team life, you also find yourself exposed for the person you really are. Peter came to Jesus and asked, "Lord, how many times shall I forgive my brother or sister who sins against me? Up to seven times?" Jesus answered, "I tell you, not seven times, but seventy-seven times."[24] By this he was not giving a mathematical formula for forgiveness. He meant we have to go on forgiving without limit, and in a team this is essential.

Some people say, "I do not suffer fools." But in team life, if you are to be of any use to God, you may have to suffer a lot of fools – or you may be one yourself!

---

[23] John 13:34-35
[24] Matthew 18:21-22

I found that one can love and be very close to people one does not agree with, providing they agree on the fundamentals of what the gospel is and have a desire to serve God with all their might. Susan, whom I had met during the training conference, summed it up when she said to a group of us, "There are some things that I would not say to George because I know that he would find it offensive." I never asked her what she meant, and if I had I expect she would not have answered. I respected her all the more for saying what she did, for it meant that she loved and respected me enough not to offend me. Our friendship meant more to her than any opinions she held to. That is the mark of a true sister or brother.

29

Treading the Boards

I had the love for film and theatre instilled in me during my youth. As mentioned previously, I had joined the local amateur theatre company. First I attended a reading and was asked to take some small parts in a play. I quickly discovered that getting into the costume transformed me into another person. I became a king and I felt like it. I was out in front of an audience with my young queen and it was as if the audience were my subjects. I loved it.

It was during the run of the play that I was asked to be in another play. I accepted. A play had been written by a very well known playwright and for a short time it was only available to the amateur theatre. I was to play a Glasgow truck driver who wanted to be a night club singer and if his father had ever found out about that then he would have belted him. He was divorced and his wife had put him down at every opportunity. All in all, he felt bad about himself, except when he sang. The character did a lot of swearing, but I decided that such a man *would* swear and in reality be much worse than he was in the script, so I did not protest about the words. They made the character credible. On the surface the character seemed hard, but when he revealed how he had been treated, I thought that the audience would warm to him, as he was not really hard at all. He loved singing and I had to sing for the performance while shouting at one of the other characters.

A big challenge was at the end of Act One where my character had a fit and ran off the stage. It was a complete mental breakdown. I did my best to simulate a panic. The character would return in the Second Act to reveal the truth about himself and I wanted the audience to react emotionally to him when they knew that the hard exterior was only to protect himself and that underneath he was a more fragile character.

Having seen the panic at the end of Act One, I heard the audience gasp each night when I came on for the Second Act. That gasp confirmed to me that I had got the panic just right, and now the audience were gripped and wondered what the character would do next. They would not be disappointed.

On my way to the stage, stewards would ask me, "Are you going to do the shouting now?" The fact that they asked this confirmed to me that they enjoyed the action very much. Alternating between shouting in a bad temper and breaking off to sing at the same time was not simple and required a lot of direction to get the emotional aspects right. I loved doing it. I felt that I had power over the audience to make them feel the way that I wanted them to feel.

I continued to play small parts and do a lot of prop handling. Even a small part can be very rewarding. I played a mentally ill man in a well-known American play. I wandered up and down continually at the back of the stage, snatching at imaginary flies and eating them, picking up books and putting them down so that the audience would feel uneasy. My character saw people who were not there, so to indicate this, I kept looking out to the audience as though I were looking at a person, with a glazed look in my eyes. This must have worked as I later found out that there was a lady in the audience who dreaded me catching her eye. When I discovered this, I was very pleased indeed. I do not consider myself to be a great actor, but I think I have a modest talent for it.

Costume dramas are amazing, I have found. Just being in the costume makes me feel great. We did 'Pride and Prejudice' which I loved. I played Sir William Lucas and it was my character who introduced Elizabeth Bennet to Mr Darcy at the Netherfield ball. When I looked at myself in a mirror in the blue tunic with long tails, the frilly shirt, the white trousers and the long boots, I thought I looked regal. We had to learn to do regency dancing.

It was like being back at secondary school when the Gym teachers told the boys to go down to the girls' gym. When we got there we were told to line up against the wall bars. The girls lined up on the other side of the room. The boys' teacher was the Head of Department and he had all his female members of staff in the gym. He told us that we needed to learn to dance for the upcoming school dance. Then he said, "Boys, take your partners." We all stood there in silence. No one moved. All of us were wondering who would go first. I thought that if I did not do something, I would get the ugliest girl in class, so I strode across the room and asked my friend Jane to dance. I found that I enjoyed dancing lessons in the weeks to come. I am not great at it, but I know enough to get by and it has proved to be a good life tool. When I am in a play that requires dancing, in my mind I am back at school in the girls' gym, once again learning to dance. I have discovered that other people of my age did not have the compulsory dancing or music lessons that I had, which has surprised me. I have now been in plays where mature adults have had to learn things that I was taught when I was twelve years old. The more I see them learn, the more I am twelve years old again.

I was getting to know the people in the theatre. I found that this brought balance to my life. I loved them more than I could have imagined and have become very good friends with them. People in a Christian organisation come to the office, go to church, and it is easy to spend all one's time with Christians. The theatre gives me what most people get in the workplace – a window to the world and all their life concerns (e.g. relationships, ageing parents) without Christ. Death is a difficult subject, for without Jesus there is no hope. When they talk about someone who has died, they will talk about the things they did for the theatre but then there is a silence. It is the elephant in the room that no one mentions. Everyone is wondering, what has become of the soul of the deceased? But no one actually asks the question. It is as though they are putting it off as they know that one day they too will die and they have no idea what lies ahead.

At a Christmas party, I attempted to remedy this. I wrote a sketch for myself in which I played all the characters. It was my own testimony of how I met Jesus Christ. The party gave me the opportunity to do this and I took it. I left it in God's hands as to what impact that would make. I know that it touched one person in particular, but as for the rest that remains to be seen. I feel that I am called to be faithful to God in what I do, but to leave the results to him.

I love the theatre because it has given me friends of both genders and all ages with different experiences of life, and they have come from other parts of the country and settled in the West Midlands. When one is alone, one's social life is very important, and the theatre has met that need for me as I have the chance to go out to meals and parties with them, and get to know them outside of the theatre for the people they are. I trust that they similarly feel that they have got to know me as a man. I believe that I have gained their trust and respect. I also hope that when they look at me, they see me as different to anyone else they know. I hope that my life reflects Christ to them and that what I say about matters of faith is credible to them because of my life.

I learned many skills. I found that I enjoy being Stage Manager because it makes me part of the team. I enjoy the integration with other people. Being Stage Manager does require some degree of skill with people. For any performance the cast will have some feeling of nerves and the thing that nobody wants is to have a Stage Manager who annoys them, and so I try to be calm and cheerful as I usher them to the stage and see to it that they all have their props. Having been on the stage myself, I empathise with them.

Most people in the company are amateurs, but there are a few on the fringe of the professional theatre. One man performs as an amateur but is a professional writer. One of the ladies is a retired actress while another man is a semi-retired actor. There are also those who have practical skills in building sets, painting and putting curtains up. It is all team work, with a view to putting on a production that is of a very high standard, and it is this attitude that I appreciate about the theatre. We want things to look good. The audience know what to expect so they keep coming back, knowing that a lot of work has gone into the performance to transport them to another world for a couple of hours.

I have found that some of the most forthright people in the company are the ones that I feel closest to. I seem to have something that they love, and they seem to enjoy my company as much as I do theirs. However, they are also a reminder to me that they are lost without Christ. I pray for them, I try to witness to them, and I want to see them in God's kingdom. God has given me insights that they do not have as yet. A spiritualist came to the theatre. I was not there but I heard about it later. A lady who was a steward could not make her mind up if he was a good conjurer or the real thing. This is a trick of the devil as both questions are wrong. We know that a conjurer does not do real tricks. He is false, and a spiritualist will give false hope. If they really are in contact with spirits then they are in contact with demons, and that is dangerous for we are forbidden in scripture to try to contact the dead. If one has trusted in Christ, one's eternal destiny is assured: we will be with Christ and that is all we need to know. If one dies in one's sins, then one is lost and faces God's wrath. We know this because the Bible says so. The spiritualist will always take us away from that, for they themselves are people who are lost and deceived by the devil.

Every season, I find myself looking forward to seeing old friends again and working with them on a production. As new people join, I like getting to know them. Each one is another person who needs Christ, even if as yet they do not know it.

30

Austria

As my overseas mission experience to date had not been with Operation Mobilisation, I decided that it would be a good idea to go on an OM short term mission one summer. I opted to go to Austria.

The first few days there were a training conference, to teach us something of the Austrian culture. Most of the participants came from Germany. We worked in conjunction with the Open Air Campaigners. They taught us how to do sketch boards. By using an easel and a board with paper, one can paint pictures as one is talking to people in the street. Most people are curious. If they see someone painting a picture, they will stop to look at it. When a number of people have stopped, the painter starts to speak to them as they continue to paint simple pictures consisting of lines and circles. The painter works to a script to tell the story he or she is illustrating. Somehow it seemed to me that doing the sketch board made talking to a crowd in shopping centres so much easier.

I went with a number of people to Villach in the South of Austria. It was very hot all the time we were there. As I do not speak German, I had something of a handicap. Nevertheless, I did the sketch board in English. I enjoyed it, and who knows if someone who spoke English as their second language was impacted by it?

The two men from the Open Air Campaigners were German. One of them told us a story to illustrate why it is important to always have some children's leaflets when you are on the streets. He said that he was out doing sketch board when a woman approached him.

"You do not recognise me, do you?" she began.

"No," he admitted.

She said, "Two years ago, you were out on the streets doing this, and I was not interested in what you had to say, but you gave a leaflet for my daughter. When we got home, I read it and I became a Christian. Two weeks later, so did my husband and we started a church meeting."

This was such an encouraging story to all of us!

There is a slight antipathy between the Austrians and the Germans. When one of the men from the Open Air Campaigners was doing sketch board, a crowd gathered and they talked among themselves. One of the girls who was part of our team said that some people in the crowd were saying, "Why is that rich German preaching to us?" He was certainly not rich but this was the perception some had of Germans.

The men on our team were staying with a family. The man was Austrian and his wife was English. She said to us, of the Austrians, "They have no sense of their own identity because of the war." I was saddened by this. I had seen how the Dutch were affected by the war, even two generations after the end of it. Here I was in a nation that had been on the other side, and deep down they still felt its consequences.

By culture, Austria is Roman Catholic. The team I was part of were working with a Baptist Church. There were about twenty in the congregation. The pastor warned us that they were considered to be a sect; that is what the Roman Catholic priests told the people. We all experienced this when an Englishman on the team suggested that we put a table outside the church building and give away tea and coffee to passers-by to engage them in conversation about Jesus. In view of what the pastor had said, I did not think this would work, but the only way to find out was to try. We spent all afternoon trying to meet people and many did pass by, but on the other side of the street! They gave us a wide berth. Only one elderly lady stopped to speak to us. She told us that she spoke five languages. During the occupation she had been a secretary to the British Army because she could speak to the officers. She knew some of the people who were passing by, and she said to us, "They will not come to you. They think you are a sect. I know you are not, but they think you are."

31

Stop the World so I Can Get Off

I was curious to see the ship's office in Germany. I sent mail to it and every four months I sent out the ship's newsletter. I knew that the ship's office and the OM Germany office were on the same site in Mosbach. It was suggested to me that I could take a holiday there as the OM Germany office was also a conference centre, and I thought this was a good idea.

I found that it was a very attractive town with wooden, highly-coloured shutters on the windows, and there were hanging baskets of flowers everywhere. It was just beautiful. I went out in the sunshine every day just to look at the town. The site of the office was a former mill, and only a short walk from the town centre. There was a dining room in which the staff of OM Germany, the ship's office and guests all ate. The meals were delicious!

I had taken some reading material with me for my evenings in the mill. I was sitting reading when the phone rang. It was the housekeeper. She told me to ring my brother; it was important. I put the phone down. "Something must have happened to my parents," I thought, with the final words, "It is important," ringing in my head.

I called my brother and he related some bad events concerning our mother that had taken place the day before. He then moved on to tell me what had happened that very day: "Mum had a heart attack and she died." This was the very news that I had been dreading.

I had to return to Dunfermline as quickly as possible. I found that cancelling my return coach journey for an earlier one was very difficult. I told the housekeeper that I had to cut the holiday short and, as I felt that I had got to know her a bit, I told her why. She related the news to the German field leader, who asked me how I was going to get back. I told him that I only had money for a coach trip and I was finding it hard to move the date of the return trip forward.

He said, "Your family need you. I will tell my secretary to book a flight to Edinburgh."

I already knew his secretary as she had spent a short time with my own team. She had been the mailroom manager on the Logos 2. She booked a flight and the next day I flew to Edinburgh.

My brother met me at the airport and drove me to Dunfermline. When we got to the house, my father burst into tears and I hugged him.

We set about arranging the funeral. Dad bought a black suit for me. It seemed like he spent money like water on the funeral.

"She is worth every penny," he said. "I have many happy memories of your mum."

A large man showed us into an office where we chose the coffin and made the final arrangements. We also arranged to go to the parlour to see Mum's body. As we sat there with my mother's body lying in the coffin, Dad spoke as though he was speaking directly to her.

"Hello darling," he began. "Forty years ago, you and me said, 'We'll make a go of it.'"

My parents had in fact been married for forty-three years, and the fortieth anniversary had been marked by the purchase of a large piece of furniture. Dad had said they would have a celebration in case they did not make it to fifty years.

I received a letter from an elderly man in my little English church. His name was Gordon. I felt that over a period of two years

I had grown close to him. I knew that he understood the pain that my family and I were going through because he had experienced it himself and, as a pastor, he had presided over many funerals. In the letter he said that when a parent dies, one's mind goes back to when we were totally dependent on them. He was right. It was as though he could read my mind.

On the day of the funeral, I looked around the church at the furniture. I recognised the choir chairs as being the same ones that had been in the church I had grown up in. We buried Mum and after a few days I went home.

Two months later, my brother phoned me. He said that he had been talking to Dad's doctor. Dad only had a short time to live. He estimated about six months. We knew that he had suffered from cancer as he had previously had an operation to remove it. The operation had been successful, but now the cancer had returned and it was terminal. We were still in the early process of grieving for our mother. "Oh God, how could you do this?" I thought.

I decided to make the best use of the time that we had. I went to stay with Dad every two weeks. My brother and his wife had two daughters and a baby son. It was thought best not to tell the girls about their grandfather's illness until it was absolutely necessary. I would arrive in Dunfermline very late on Friday evening and see Dad in the morning. As the weeks went by, I could see that he was becoming weaker. We knew that the coming Christmas would be the last we would ever spend with him.

On Christmas Day Dad gave me a gift. As I accepted it and held it in my arms, I thought, "This will be the last gift Dad ever gives me." It was a very thick, purple jersey – something just right for December. I discovered that when you know someone close to you is terminally ill, the grieving starts even while they are still with you.

I continued to go to Dunfermline every two weeks. One Saturday morning Dad came into the room and I could see there was a marked decline in his condition compared to the last time I had seen him. His voice had grown weak. I thought, "We cannot keep this from the girls any longer; the look of him is enough to tell anyone that he is gravely ill. I must go round to my brother's house and tell him that we must talk to the girls now." When I got there, I found that the older girl had already worked it out. It was such a relief to be able to talk about the situation in front of her without having to disappear into a bedroom to talk in private. The six months the doctor gave Dad came and went, and he was still alive. However, we still knew that his death was inevitable. He had told the doctor that he was sure of where he was going. He had put his trust in Christ. This was something that I had prayed for over a number of years. God had answered my prayer.

The day came when I was at work and I received a call from the doctor. It is unusual for general practitioners to make long distance calls, so I knew what he was about to say. The doctor told me that Dad had been admitted to hospital and I should come now. The next day I set off for Dunfermline and went with my family to see him. The next day he died. Once again, Gordon sent me a very kind letter. He said that there is something so final when the second parent dies. That is exactly how I felt. I also thought that no matter how we present it, death is always an ugly business. We buried him in the same grave as our mother.

I went to the USA to visit Katie, whom I had met when I joined OM. When she left our team, she went to Pasadena to work in mission there. I asked her if I could come and visit her, and she agreed. She saw to it that I could stay in a house with other men whom she worked with. So I flew into Los Angeles, and Katie drove me to the house where I was going to stay.

On the 4th of July, I went with some of the men to a fairground. I played a game on one of the stalls and won an enormous Tweety-Pie bird which I posted to myself as it was too large to take on the plane going home!

On another day, at the house, we all had to help ourselves from a plate of rice in the middle of the table. I stuck the wooden spoon into the rice, but it would not come off the spoon. I shook it and it still would not budge. To my surprise, some of the men round the table became alarmed. I could see the shock on their face and they were audibly gasping. They could see what was about to follow. The only way I could get the rice off the spoon was to hit the plate with it. But as soon as I did that, another man round the table panicked. He reached over, grabbed the spoon and ran off into the kitchen to wash it. I realised from this that everyone living in the house had to tolerate this one's unusual compulsive behaviour.

I was presented with an opportunity to speak to people who worked in the mission. Katie told me that they rarely had visitors from Europe so I would probably appeal to them. I addressed the meeting and gave them a broad view of the work in Europe, including the things that I had been involved in. The Americans were very receptive.

There are things that in Europe are commonplace but less so in the USA. The mission had some visitors, people who were considering joining, and I sat in on one of the meetings. At the end of the day we all went to an Indian restaurant. I have been to many Indian restaurants in the UK, but these people had never been to one. I was intrigued by the excitement of young ladies eating chicken wings. One of them handed me one and said, "Try that!" I decided not to spoil her moment of excitement by telling her that I had eaten them many times. For her it was a new and thrilling experience.

Because of my love for movies, I went with one of the other men along the Hollywood Walk of Fame. It was not quite what I expected. I thought the paving stones with the stars' names on them could do with a clean and there was at least one man in the street wearing woman's clothes. However, it was great to go and see the latest Star Wars film. The audience took to their feet at the end and gave a round of applause. It was a great atmosphere. I also went with Katie to the Universal studios. I purchased a Crocodile Dundee style bush hat, which in the UK is not just helpful in the summer, it is great at keeping the rain and snow off my head in the winter as well.

32

The Passing Years

As the years went by, and people on the team came and went, a lot of changes took place. The team grew larger as we took on more work and I formed new friendships. Sometimes it felt like being in a soap opera. The story goes on and it does not end, but the characters change, except for just a few. I think new people bring with them new energy to the work. Some people did not leave the team but they changed their positions in the team. Doing so refreshed them.

To anyone observing us, it would appear that we do office work. If anyone were to watch me, they would say, "He sends out letters and magazines." Indeed I do, but when I look back on the time I received the letters, they made a difference to me and eventually brought me here. It was a letter that helped me do my first short term mission and it was the inspiration of a book followed by a friend's request that got me to Amsterdam. As I send out letters and magazines, I know that there are many people for whom it is just the thing they need and some will come into the work. Some will support it, some will pass it on to someone else and they will respond to it.

One of our team members tells a story of two men breaking stones. A man goes up to the first and asks, "What are you doing?"

"Can you not see?" he replies. "I am breaking stones."

The man then goes to the second and asks, "What are *you* doing?"

"Can you not see?" he replies. "I am building temples."

It is all a matter of how we look at things. I am doing my part in building God's kingdom. If I did not believe that, I would not do it.

Over the years, I have given regular Bible teaching to the team. I love doing it. When I teach, I believe that I am building God's kingdom first of all in my own life, and second in the lives of others. I have also discovered the value of prayer more and more. There is indeed corporate prayer, but it is also important to have personal prayer. What I have with God is a father and son relationship. He is my heavenly Father and I am an adopted son. I can talk to him any time of the day or night. Often these are times of thanks to God for what he has done for me or what he has given me. God likes to be thanked. It is showing appreciation and love to him. I can even look back now and thank him for difficult things that have proved to be good for me. Jesus himself prayed often to his heavenly Father and he taught the disciples to do likewise. He taught them to ask for forgiveness for sin. I have done that many times and I expect to go on doing that until the day I die, for no matter how much I contend against the sin within me, I am still a sinner – but I also have the Holy Spirit in me. There is a struggle between the two natures within me and because of my weakness, sometimes I give in and God knows it. God knows everything. As a father asks a naughty son to explain his actions, so God expects me to come to him when I have sinned and ask for forgiveness. He has promised to give more of the Holy Spirit to those who ask, and this is a lesson that I am still learning.

Most Christmases I go to my brother and sister-in-law's house and celebrate with them. Christmas 1999 was no exception. After the celebrations, they then went to Glasgow to her parents for the New Year, leaving me alone in the house.

I had decided to attend a party at the church. I thought that this would probably be the last time that I would do this. I had attended many such parties when I lived in the town, and I wanted to celebrate this with people whom I had known for many years. As usual, I had a lovely time. It was a time of thankfulness to God for the years he had given, and we looked forward to what he would do in the future. There was a feeling of excitement. At the end of the party I went back to the house and sat down to watch the New Year celebrations on television.

The phone rang. I picked it up. It was my cousin Ian. He told me that his mother, my Aunt Chrissie, had died that day. I hung up and remembered how my Aunt Margaret had always dreaded being the last of her own family, and now it had actually happened. I was glad that I had been in the house that night to receive the news, but I knew that I had a daunting task to perform. I was going to have to tell Aunt Margaret about her sister's death.

I called my brother and broke the news him, and told him that I would go and see Aunt Margaret. In the morning I went to the respite home where she was staying for a short time. As I entered the building, I spoke to two of the staff and told them what I was about to do, and asked them to keep an eye on her when I left. She was pleased to see me, but her face fell when I broke the news and she went silent. The news hit her hard. I stayed and spoke to her as she ventured to break her silence. She said that she would not be able to go to the funeral. I said, "We will wait and see." Emotionally it was too much for her.

This was not the start to the Millennium that I had imagined. In the days to come the funeral was arranged. Aunt Chrissie was to be cremated. I had gone home but returned to Dunfermline for the funeral. Aunt Margaret did not make the emotional recovery that I had hoped and, as she had said, she was in no fit state to attend. My brother and I went. Aunt Chrissie's former minister conducted the funeral. She had been a matriarchal figure in our lives and now she was gone. It was the end of an era.

33

Babs

I had spent my life alone. This was not a deliberate choice and I had on several occasions joined an organisation looking for a life companion. So far I had not found one, but now I did meet someone who was vastly different to anyone else. I wrote to an African woman in London, called Babs. Over a number of weeks we exchanged a number of letters and photographs and we agreed to meet. I decided that it would be best if I went by coach and she should meet me at the Victoria Coach Station. As I sat on the coach, I wondered what she would be like. One gets an impression from letters, but that is only usually only a shadow of what that person is like.

I got off the coach and looked around. There seemed to be no sign of her. Had she backed out at the last moment and decided not to come, I wondered? Then I heard a voice calling my name. I turned around and there was a cute little black woman smiling at me. We greeted one another and we had coffee together at the coach station. The conversation was somewhat stilted. I wanted to know how she had got into a bad relationship. She said that she had got into it because she had been blind. She meant that she had been spiritually blind but now she could see.

We went to the hostel where she was living. In the conversation that followed, I reached the conclusion that she was a recent convert. She had been in a relationship that had broken down and left the house that had been her home. Her sisters had helped her move out and the hostel was a temporary place to live. I asked her how long she had been in the country. She produced certificates that proved she had residency. I had not intended this. I thought that I was just making conversation, showing an interested in her life. She thought that I was wondering if she was an illegal immigrant. In spite of our differences, I found her to be an interesting woman.

Being a single parent was exhausting for her. Early one evening as we sat watching TV, she fell asleep in my arms. It was a tender moment as I sat there doing my best not to move and wake her. She worked very hard at being a good parent. I admired and respected her for that. However, the differences between us proved too much.

I did continue to send her Christmas cards. From time to time we would still meet up, and on one occasion we met in Edinburgh and I took her to meet my family. I found that I admired her all the more as she continued to grow in faith and to get qualifications as a cook and catering manager. We still had vast differences, but I could see more things from her point of view. I loved her optimism. I am more pragmatic, and sometimes it is helpful to have someone who is the opposite as a counterbalance. I enjoyed that. I noticed that she had no sense of what I called fun. There was no feeling of getting into a relationship one step at a time. I felt under pressure that this was to go all the way to marriage or not at all, and that 'slowly but surely' was not on her agenda. I think this was the main cultural difference between us. There would be long periods where we did not see each other, but I would sometimes write to her. I tried to reinstate the relationship on a number of occasions, but every time I came up against the same barrier: that in her culture things had to be more firm, and there had to be a long term plan and not the step-by-step that I preferred.

I told her that I am a much more conservative Christian than her. I do not think she took on board what that meant. There are all sorts of churches and I knew that hers would reflect her culture. It was at one church meeting that she felt that she had to introduce me to the pastor, for he had said that if you cannot introduce your friends to your pastor then there is something wrong. I agreed to this. I knew that hers was a 'suit' church. In my churches we had long stopped wearing suits to church as people did when I was a child. But I took a suit for this occasion. The church rented a building from a Bible college. As I expected, I was the only white person there. There was a severely disabled girl in a wheelchair and a lot of children. At the start of the meeting there was a young woman at the front singing her heart out. She was an amazing singer. There was a lot of congregational singing that followed and then a sermon. An image was projected on to a screen. I had seen photos of the founder of the church, and the video on the screen was him preaching about giving. At the end an offering was taken up.

The meeting came to a close and it had been agreed in advance that I would meet the pastor. While I was waiting, all visitors were asked to sit together and a young woman gave us forms to fill in. It was like being in business, where you were expected to fill all your contact details in. I did not want to give offence, so I filled it in, but it felt awkward. I have no objection to filling in a visitor's book, but this was more than that. One of the questions was, "Do you speak in tongues?" and there were 'Yes' or 'No' boxes to tick. The next question was, "If you ticked, 'No', would you like to?" and again there were two tick boxes. I pondered on the day of Pentecost and how the Holy Spirit had enabled people to speak in other languages, but it seemed to me that they had no choice in the matter. They suddenly found they could speak in other languages. According to the form I had in my hand, it seemed to me that they thought that I could choose. I do not think that is the case. In fact it was a sign to unbelieving Jews, and it was God's judgement on them that they refused to believe and now he was conferring his blessing on all who would believe. They also asked me where I lived, and when I replied they said that the nearest church in their organisation was in Birmingham – which is a long way. I pointed out that I already was in a church near my home.

Babs came to me and said, "The pastor is ready for us." There was a booking system to see the pastor and our time had come. The three of us sat down and talked. He asked if we wanted to get married. Babs and I had agreed in advance that this would only be a meeting to tell him that we were still getting to know one another. I told him about the mission work I did. Babs remained silent throughout the meeting; the pastor and I did all the talking. It seemed polite and formal to me.

I invited Babs to Dunfermline to meet my brother, his wife and their son over Easter. I drove to Dunfermline, while she caught a train to Edinburgh. I decided that it would be simplest if I took a train from Dunfermline to Edinburgh to meet her there.

I had no idea what time I could get a train to Edinburgh, but I parked the car at the station and caught the first train that came by. Upon arrival, it was just like our first meeting – I could not see Babs and had to search for her. I walked all over the concourse and went into a cafeteria. There she was, at one of the tables, waving at me. We greeted one another and found the time of the next train back to Dunfermline.

The meeting with my family seemed to go okay. I wondered what Babs thought. We all went to my Dunfermline church on Easter Sunday. How different it must have seemed to her to her own church. Hers had many more people in it; the building could not hold them all.

At the end of the weekend, it was time to for Babs to go home. She remarked on how my brother was very quiet and my sister-in-law was very nice. I thought that this was the best that I could expect. Once again, however, I felt there was a barrier between us. We could not just relax and enjoy the relationship. We did not see each other for some time, but I got in touch with her. Some emails were exchanged between us. Eventually I decided that I wanted to have things settled one way or another. By now we were sending text messages. In one of them she said that she was considering returning to her own country. I wrote a letter telling her that I did not want her to and asked her how firm that plan was. We agreed to meet. I resolved in my mind that this time, whatever the outcome, it would be final.

I drove to her place, and when I got there, I found that one of her sisters was visiting. We had the discussion that I had come for. The only thing that surprised me was that her sister was part of the conversation – but I had no objection. While Babs was out of the room her sister told me of her concerns. I tried to reassure her that I had thought of the cultural differences between us and that I would not want to see Babs unhappy. If it meant finding a group of African people to fellowship with then I would be happy to do that.

Babs returned to the room and they asked me, "What is your plan?" I really should not have been surprised at this, but I was. Here it was again, the same barrier. They wanted a long-term, detailed plan, when I needed to go step-by-step. I could see from the expression on their faces that this mystified them and this was not the answer they wanted. Babs reminded me of the day we met her pastor and said that I had told him that we were getting to know one another, yet here we were some time later, still at that point. I knew she was right about that. The difference was that I had one way of getting beyond that point and she had another. She then said that we could be friends, we could call and text one another, but I was not ready. I said nothing as I could not see any point in continuing the discussion. Things were now confirmed in my mind. We were never going to get beyond the barrier, so I left things at that. I had resolved that this would be final.

When I got home, I sent a text to Babs to let her know that I was safe. I also determined in my heart to look for someone else more suitable for me. The cultural issues between us had proved too great, but I felt that I had benefited from the relationship, and I am so grateful to God for bringing Babs into my life.

34

The Fields are White

When one is in mission work, it is very noticeable that over a number of years things change. The world is a harvest field and there are so many opportunities, but there are never sufficient workers. We can never say we have enough workers; there is need for more. In the years I have been in mission, the work has greatly expanded and both the team and the office building are considerably larger.

A great deal of planning went into expanding the office. I would see the builders every day digging trenches to lay the foundations of the extension. Things largely went to plan, but there had to be some minor changes to it. It had been decided that new drains were needed outside my flat. The new building would go up first. One day I noticed flooding and upon further inspection, it was discovered that concrete had leaked into the drain and blocked it. The plan for the new drain had to be brought forward, to avoid further flooding.

Sometimes I would chat to the builders. They were a hardy bunch. I admired them for working in all sorts of weather – rain, hail or shine. I would not like that, but for them it was not a problem. One of them caught a heavy cold but he was back at work the next day. I am not so sure that I would make such a speedy recovery.

Some demolition was required. The office had once been a Barnardos school and when the plaster was taken off one of the walls, it revealed shower tiles behind it. I was also told that the present mailroom was once a dining room. A large hole was made in one of the exterior walls of the staff room where the extension would be. It was boarded up for the duration of the building project. Not only did the boards keep out the wind and the rain, they also kept out intruders during the night.

Over a period of months the extension was erected and I was given keys to it. As I held those new keys in my hand and looked at the building, I had a sense of the future. The extension was a necessity for what we as a team would be doing in the years to come. We had prayed and looked to God for the money for the extension and God had granted it. I felt like I was part of something big and glorious, for which I thanked God. We would be doing more work for God to reach those who as yet do not know him. How many people throughout the world would get to hear of his love and mercy as a result of the extension of the office? I expect that I will only get to know the answer to that when I see the Lord. I am convinced, however, that much is now being done for the kingdom of God that would not have happened without the extension, and God is enabling us to do it for his glory.

Afterword

Sometimes I look back, and I can see a pattern in my life, like a kaleidoscope, that I was not aware of at the time. All the colours and shapes were changing, and yet merging into one. All the aspects of my life have merged into one purpose, and that is to broadcast the gospel.

The church I grew up in closed and I then went to another church where I got the Bible teaching that I had lacked up until then. Not only did I receive the teaching, I found the minister inspiring, and it was he who encouraged me to preach for the first time, which I have been doing ever since. If the church I grew up in had not closed, I would never have made the move to other one. Clearly this was in God's providence for me, to teach and to train me.

It was when I was attending a Bible study that I was asked if I would like to go to visit a Christian ship. I thought that would be exciting so I went. That ship was the Doulos. I had no concept then that one day I would be a part of the organisation that ran the ship. It was a link God used to get me to where I am now.

It was at university that I approached David and asked him where he got the sermon recordings from that he played when we met in his flat. I did not know that by getting the contact details, I was making my first direct contact with the organisation that I am now a part of.

It is now that I see this was all God's providence. Through these circumstances he was revealing more and more of himself to me, and he continues to do so. My life is still unfolding like the kaleidoscope colours.

Yes, God's grace is amazing, but we only realise how amazing it is when we know the depth of our sin, how we have offended him and that he has not poured out his wrath upon us as we deserve. We have a problem in the West. Often we do not think we are sinners. We are noted for being decadent. We say we are not perfect, but we have no concept of sin. We do not recognise the gravity of our true situation. We are blind. We go about life treating it as okay, believing that when we die we will not be giving an account to God for the way we have lived the life that he gave us. We think that life is ours and we have rights. In fact, we have been given life by God and we do not have rights; we have responsibilities before God as to what we do with it.

Many Christians I have known, who have influenced me for good, have now passed into eternity. I miss them but I look forward to seeing them again one day. One of them, as he was dying, said, "Heaven is bright." I know that my sins are forgiven and now I have to live for the Lord, laying aside sin. It is difficult but I owe him everything I am; so for my saviour nothing it too much. I find that struggling with sin, mastering it, does not get easier, and it may raise its ugly head when I do not expect it, but master it I must. I can only do that by submitting to God; there is no other way of doing it.

I look forward to the things that are yet to come: the people God will bring across my path who need to hear the gospel and be saved, or who have a message for me that will inspire me to go on to more and more service in Jesus Christ. I have always found that God surprises me and he may have more in store. I am a student. I learn from God, and I expect to go on learning. There may be hard lessons and there may be pleasant lessons, but I need to be willing to learn in all circumstances.

I need to go on being renewed and saying to God, "Take my life and let it be consecrated, Lord, to thee."

This is my prayer for my life. Is it yours?

AMEN. Let it be.